QUEERS WERE HERE:
HEROES & ICONS OF QUEER CANADA

Queers Were Here:
Heroes & Icons of Queer Canada

ROBIN GANEV AND RJ GILMOUR

BIBLIOASIS
WINDSOR, ONTARIO

FIRST EDITION

Library and Archives Canada Cataloguing in Publication

Queers were here / Robin Ganev and Richard Gilmour, editors.

Issued in print and electronic formats.
ISBN 978-1-77196-086-1 (paperback).--ISBN 978-1-77196-087-8 (ebook)

1. Sexual minorities--Canada--History. 2. Sexual minorities--Canada. 3. Gays--Canada--History. 4. Gays--Canada.

I. Ganev, Robin, 1973-, editor II. Gilmour, R. J. (Richard James), 1964-, editor

HQ73.3 C3 Q4 2016   306.76'60971   C2016-901170-4
                                                 C2016-901171-2

Canada Council   Conseil des Arts   Canadian   Patrimoine
for the Arts   du Canada   Heritage   canadien

ONTARIO ARTS COUNCIL
CONSEIL DES ARTS DE L'ONTARIO
50 YEARS OF ONTARIO GOVERNMENT SUPPORT OF THE ARTS
50 ANS DE SOUTIEN DU GOUVERNEMENT DE L'ONTARIO AUX ARTS

Biblioasis acknowledges the ongoing financial support of the Government of Canada through the Canada Council for the Arts, Canadian Heritage, the Canada Book Fund; and the Government of Ontario through the Ontario Arts Council and the Ontario Media Development Corporation.

Edited by Jeer Heer
Copy-edited by Allana Amlin
Cover Illustration by John Webster
Typeset and designed by Chris Andrechek

PRINTED AND BOUND IN CANADA

MIX
Paper from
responsible sources
FSC   FSC® C004071
www.fsc.org

Contents

You may forget but

*Let me tell you
this: someone in
some future time
will think of us.*
—Sappho

Introduction

*All sorrows can be borne if you put them into a story or tell a
story about them.*

—Isak Dinesen

A young man finds love and acceptance in the vibrant
queer scene of Toronto's Church Street in the 1980s.
The scion of an elite, Upper Canadian family abandons the
safety of tony Rosedale to run off to Mexico with his young
lover, sparking an international manhunt. A teenage girl
from a conservative Catholic family moves to Nelson, BC,
to go to art school, where she is surprised to find a large,
lively, unapologetic queer community. A high-school student, whose body exhibits both male and female characteris-
tics, is transformed when he discovers the eye-opening work
of Marie Claire-Blais through an inspiring English teacher.
These are some of the stories told in *Queers Were Here*, a
book about queer sexuality in Canada.

We asked queer writers of diverse backgrounds to create
a portrait of a person who had a profound influence on their
understanding of their sexuality. Our guiding purpose was the
conviction that queer pioneers who challenged the dominant
culture and fought for greater tolerance needed to be remembered and celebrated. The essays serve as a bridge: a current
generation of writers honour their role models, and younger

LGBTQ people would, hopefully read these essays, creating a conversation between past and present. We left the precise choice of subject up to the authors. Some focused on well-known activists, some on ordinary men and women, some on organizations. The range of voices and subjects makes for a rich tapestry that captures the past and present of the Canadian queer community and culture since the 1970s.

Despite the variety of perspectives, the essays address a number of common themes that offer valuable insights into queer culture. Many queer men and women had to contend with conservative families and communities who had little sympathy for their sexuality. Being different was a struggle. Scott Symons was the descendent of an old, elite Canadian family. His rebellion against sexual repression in the late 1960s was all the more outrageous because of his illustrious background. Nancy Jo Cullen's family was middle-class, but they were conservative Catholics in Kelowna, BC, a stodgy town in the 1980s. Cullen's fear of her family's reaction to her lesbian sexuality made her live in denial about who she was until her 30s.

Queer lives illustrate how being different sexually is related to being artistically inclined. This, in part, explains the motivation of the members of General Idea, the collective that used art to explore gay themes in the 1970s and 1980s. The work of General Idea was widely appreciated, because they worked in a large city. But smaller towns and rural communities did not always react well to aspiring artists or writers. For Alec Butler, being different made self-expression through writing incredibly attractive. As a sensitive student in a rural high school on the east coast, he loved English, especially the work of Marie Claire Blais. But his working-class family's contempt for writing made his dream of becoming a writer seem unreachable.

It is this sense of not belonging that has given rise to the idea of the Sacred Monster: the queer person as something deviant and beautiful at the same time. Scott Symons has been called a sacred monster, seeming to speak with the voice of a prophet to defend homoerotic sex as sacred, yet angry, undisciplined and uncompromising at the same time. Alec Butler saw himself as a sacred monster, because his body was neither male nor female, confusing and repelling those around him, yet he found redemption and expression for his suffering through writing and theatre.

As art and literature have shaped these identities, so has geography and a sense of place. The authors' places of origin include Winnipeg, British Columbia, the east coast, and small towns in Ontario. But most now live and work in Toronto. The history of queer Toronto comes alive in these stories. The excitement of Church Street in the 1980s, the concerts of Carole Pope, the sensational installations of General Idea—these are all expressions of Toronto's queer culture. But it was not all fun and parties: there were the bathhouse raids and the devastating impact of AIDS on the city's community.

A number of the authors cite *The Body Politic* and its later incarnation *Xtra!* as an important force in how they came to terms with their queer identities. In the age of digital media we must remember how print magazines like *The Body Politic* and *Xtra!* were lifelines for young people across Canada. Nik Sheehan writes how the magazine connected him to larger discussions about queer identity. Before digital media, positive representations of queers were few and hard to find in mainstream media.

The product of a collective group of activists, the history of *The Body Politic* is the history of queer Canada. Founded in 1971 in the wake of Stonewall, the magazine gave voice to a generation of activists who wanted to change how lesbians and gay men were perceived and represented in Canadian culture. At the same time the magazine created a community for discussion about important issues to queer Canadians. It was at once a forum for community building and an advocate for change.

Over the years *The Body Politic* reported on LGBTQ events and communities across the country, always advocating for political change while pushing the boundaries of sexuality and identity. Indeed in the 1980s *The Body Politic* fought a series of battles over obscenity that helped change broader attitudes about sexuality and identity across Canada.

As the queer community coalesced due in part to the efforts of *The Body Politic*, the 1970s collective corporatized in 1975 becoming Pink Triangle Press. In the 1990s, *The Body Politic* which was more activist and political in nature, was replaced with *Xtra!* which focused on culture and entertainment. These changes reflected larger trends in the queer community. *The Body Politic's* fight for inclusion and acceptance became in essence its own death warrant as queer communities became more mainstream in the 1990s. The politics of acceptance which defined the activism of the 1970s gave way to the purchasing power of the queer community in the 1980s and the birth of *Xtra!* in 1984. In 2015, almost 30 years later, the print edition of *Xtra!* was retired by Pink Triangle Press in favour of a new online digital platform, *Daily Xtra,* mirroring the move from print to digital by other forms of media.

Through all of its incarnations, the magazines produced by Pink Triangle Press provided not only a voice for the LGBTQ community but also a forum to feature the work of young queer authors, journalists and artists. Coming together the publications helped define, create and give voice to our community. At some point in their careers, most of our authors had their work featured in either *The Body Politic* or *Xtra!* Over its long life from 1971 to the present, the publications of Pink Triangle Press helped define and create queer culture in Canada.

Some of the essays raise difficult issues including intergenerational sex. For queer men and women, intergenerational sex is one of the ways for culture to pass from one generation to another. Maria Belen Ordonez's essay on Sharpe is perhaps the most controversial essay to address this topic, but despite some hesitation we decided it was important to allow her voice to be heard.

The impact of the AIDS epidemic and its destructive effect on the LGBTQ community is another aspect of queer history that deserves more attention. It is harrowing to read our authors' accounts of the loss of friends and loved ones. Gordon Bowness's incredible downtown queer scene was decimated. General Idea was reduced to one member. But gay activists, like Tim McCaskill, became stronger and more tightly organized in response. The gay community demanded to be heard. They educated the public about the disease. They fought for better treatment of patients, money for research, quicker approval of new drugs. In the end, the development of effective drugs against HIV is the result of all this hard-fought activism.

The stories told in this book are disparate but they trace a common arc of a generation, starting with isolated individuals becoming aware of their sexuality, learning more about it through contacts with the wider world, joining queer communities and becoming involved in the creation of a new culture and politics. As queers have won battles in the political sphere, they face a new challenge of how to maintain a cohesive identity in the face of mainstream acceptance. Surely one answer is through historical memory and recounting stories of how the community was formed. Hence, this book.

Murmurs of Desire

RJ GILMOUR

And so it was I entered the broken world
To trace the visionary company of love, its voice
An instant in the wind (I know not whither hurled)
But not for long to hold each desperate choice.
— Hart Crane, "The Broken Tower"

Growing up on the outskirts of London, a small town in Southwestern Ontario, I never doubted the notion of my own queerness because I was always drawn towards difference rather than sameness. I always felt alien, raised by earthlings who had no idea who or what I was. Small towns breed a longing for more. A curiosity of what lays beyond. My family never understood my tastes or my desires. Like Sadie Ratliff in the film *Big Business,* I looked to the stars dreaming of the day when my kind would come and take me away.

As a child I hungered for images of otherness in order to understand myself and my desires. While these representations were few and far between, I revelled in everything camp and queer. I was attracted to characters who were larger than life who made themselves glamorous by sheer force of will. Vito Russo's *The Celluloid Closet* shows how a dearth of images forces queers to make the most of what they can find. In the documentary, after a critique of films which showed gay men as fairies and queens, Harvey Fierstein states, "I liked the fairies," because while they were queer their presence made him feel less alone. I felt the same way growing up, I loved the campy humour of *H.R. Pufnstuf.* I loved the Auntie Mame's, the Divine's, the Barbra's, the Judy's. I looked forward every day to Paul Lynde's Uncle Arthur, Maurice Evans' Maurice and Agnes Moorehead's Endora on *Bewitched* and to the campy humour of Charles Nelson Reilly on *Match Game.* They were odd and queer at the same time and they let me know that I was not alone, that I was not the only freak in the village.

While queer characters like these showed up in television and films as the butt of jokes for heterosexual humour, for me their existence spoke of a world outside of my own. Through these characters I learned about a queer world that was coming into its own as I was becoming a young adult. Of course I wanted to run away to New York, the mecca for all things queer in the 1970s, but I was too young to venture there on my own. Instead I was left with a hunger, and a curiosity about what lay over the rainbow, outside of the confines of my small town. I was Dorothy Gale waiting for a tornado to whisk me off to Oz.

Anyone who is different knows that once we can, we begin the search for others from our tribe; we search out our clan. I gravitated to anyone who had a little of the dust of the outside world on their clothes. Being underage I was unable to go to bars in London but found other young gay guys in the parks and bushes where men congregated, looking for sex. Through the small group of friends I made, I learned about a gay youth group run out of the local gay organization, the Homophile Association of London Ontario (H.A.L.O.).

Homophile associations were one of the first activist organizations seeking to decriminalize and normalize homosexuality while giving lesbians and gay men places to socialize outside of clubs and bars. In London, H.A.L.O. provided not only a place for the LGBTQ community, but also bar nights, political activism and social spaces for organizations that grew out of the needs of the community. In the early days of the movement Homophile associations and their unique acronyms appeared in communities across the country filling a need as LGBTQ communities grew and developed.

The youth group that met at H.A.L.O., The London Gay Youth Association, was formed by young people to help underage queers struggling with their sexual identities. Too often, underage youth had few venues to meet in a safe environment. During the late 1970s and early 1980s, offering help to anyone under age was risky business. The gay community itself was struggling for safe places and could not risk the wrath of a homophobic society that imagined that gay men recruited.

Sadly, the lack of spaces for young people to meet meant that gay teens struggling with their sexuality ended up on the street when their families cast them out. This also led to a higher than normal suicide rate for young gay teens. I witnessed this among the friends I made in the group. While people came and went, the group became a community and when we learned about the death of one our friends, because they saw no other way out, it left us all disheartened about our own futures. At the time no one told us to hang on, "that life gets better." We were left to our own devices and in the wake of the deaths of our friends, we vowed to make sure we would help anyone who seemed lost or alone.

In the face of these problems a few brave individuals, including Richard Hudler, the president of H.A.L.O., offered the gay youth group a safe place to meet and resources for the group as it struggled to find its voice. While involved with the youth group, I met a man named Vernon Hern who was twenty years my senior. Everyone in London knew Vern, he was a political leader in the community having helped create H.A.L.O. in the 1970s and also stood out because of his penchant for leather.

In the time that Vern and I were together (we dated for four years), he helped me understand not only how queer culture developed in Canada, but also across time and space. As a young man from a farming community in Southwestern Ontario, he collected all forms of print about emerging queer communities in both Canada and the United States. He was trying to come to terms with his own identity and sexuality, in the repressive world of the late 1950s and early 1960s, and was searching for ways to find others who shared his desires.

What I was experiencing in my youth in the late 1970s and early 1980s, he experienced earlier in the late 1950s and early 1960s. While we were decades apart in age and what we had experienced, we shared common bonds as gay men coming of age in a society that refused to validate our existence.

Vern taught me a vocabulary, a language of desire to express and describe what I had always felt. He helped me come to terms with my sense of alienation and introduced me to the LGBTQ community in London and showed me how our community was connected to other gay communities in Toronto, New York, Fire Island, Provincetown, San Francisco and Chicago. He introduced me to the world of social connections through sex, showing me how the world of queer desire was fluid as sex allowed us to cross boundaries of class and race. Sex was our social lubricant. Vern embraced and celebrated everything that sexual liberation had to offer showing me how powerful sex could be.

It was exciting to travel with him to all these new places and to meet groups of men I would otherwise never have encountered. One of the most amazing things about being queer is how our sexuality allows us not only to see divisions that separate others but also to cross these borders. Desire and sex bring us together in ways that do not exist in heterosexual society. After decades of repression, LGBTQ individuals were happy to find others like themselves and to celebrate who they were.

For me Vern was Kali. He was the leather God of London, an intense, small man who seemed larger than he was. I remember how he moved; it was always with precision and thought. In my mind's eye I still see him, dark haired and dark eyed with glasses that seemed to see through everything. He danced through life destroying existing worlds while new worlds crystallized in his wake filled with magic, perversity and desire. There were no simple emotions with him, people either loved him or hated him. I found myself enraptured by the world he opened for me. He pulled me apart at the seams and left me alone to stitch myself back together, to own the needle and thread and to claim what clothed me. He had little patience for fools, little patience for rules and a love of life that was fuelled by desire.

Like the LGBTQ community as whole, when I met Vern he was filled with a heady desire for life. He wanted to taste everything and to learn as much about the world as he could. I was just thankful that I was allowed to go along for the ride. Vern made me who I am today. At the time I had no idea. I was awash with desire and eager to break the bonds of my small town. I followed where he led, excited by every door that he opened. Only over time have I come to appreciate how much he gave me. I owe him so much, and a day doesn't go by when I don't think about him and who he was. I still hear his voice in my head. His advice is always there, sometimes heeded, sometimes not. His ideas sliced away any vestiges of idealism or romanticism. He was a romantic cynic, hardened by a broken heart. At times he could be such a bastard, but he was always one step ahead of me and generously fed my voracious appetite for more.

Coming of age in the early 1960s, Vern witnessed the birth of the modern gay liberation movement. After graduating college he became a school teacher because teaching gave him his summers off, allowing him to travel to all the emerging hotspots of queerdom. He witnessed the flourishing of gay culture in the days after Stonewall in cities all across North America. In these places he found reflections of who he wanted to be. At the same time he was part of a leather community that was also discovering its own voice. Following in the wake of LGBTQ liberation, leather queens came together through their love of hyper-masculine desire and sexuality.

While trying to find himself, after a stint in a commune in North Virginia, Vern decided teaching was too limiting for an out gay man so he gave it up. Along the way he tried a number of different careers, searching for a job that gave him the freedom to explore who he was. By the time I met him he was working in a university library. He became a conduit for me to that magical queer world that existed outside of my small town.

Vern always suggested that the tenants of queer culture were passed from generation to generation through inter-generational relationships. For him, our relationship was unique. Up until he had met me, his partners were all close to him in age. He suggested that gay men passed on their knowledge, their wisdom and the language of gay culture to another generation through friendships, love and sex. Advice, hope, direction and despair were all communicated along this tricky conduit.

We didn't breed our replacements like our heterosexual counterparts but inculcated them through gesture, style and form. Coming of age in the gay community meant learning to navigate the symbols and language of being queer. After all, no matter our age or background, we share common experiences as victims of heterosexism. We know what it is like to feel alone and we all experience coming out at some point in our lives. I liked Vern's take on the idea of queer culture, it explained how some of the tenets of queer culture survived across generations and geographical borders.

Through Vern I got to know not only other gay men his age, but also men older than him. I came to know his mentors and friends who had lived in the shadows of World War II and post-war society before the days of Stonewall. Their world was so different from his and mine and yet so fascinating. From these men I learned the history of queerness and gay identity. They revelled in the camp and the ridiculous. They knew how to find fun in a world where they were never welcome. They found happiness in the darkest of places, and learned how to revel, while laughing at pain and torment.

It was an exhilarating experience for a young man trying to find himself and his own way. I was allowed into the hallowed ground of this world because I had youth on my side. A young cute face amused these older gentlemen. Sitting back I quietly soaked it up, marvelling at the verbal games and wit of their play. They had a coded language filled with film references and gestures that were swords and shields in a manner I adored. They parried and thrust using their tongues as weapons. It was like watching live theatre playing out in front of you. Through Vern and his friends I discovered a world filled with joy, laughter, camp, desire and education. The experience left me heady, with an insatiable curiosity about a world overflowing with desire.

Vern gave me a taste of what the gay world was like before 1980. I danced with the ghosts of the past and those of a future to come. As a teenager I read about this world in the pages of *The Body Politic* and William Como's *After Dark* magazine (a New York arts magazine filled with queer content that predated more openly queer periodicals). Vern let me taste the world of the 1970s, of hedonism unleashed, of desire unfulfilled and a lust that knew no boundaries. At the time he was my lover, my teacher, my best friend and a queer father.

I did not know it at the time, but I learned later that the magical world of queer desire and queer culture that I had discovered was slowly unravelling in the face of an epidemic that would decimate an entire generation. Sitting at the feet of these older men and queens I tasted a world that was evaporating. I longed for the magic they described, for the days I had never lived. I missed the worlds I savoured in the kisses and stories of Vern's friends. I tasted in their sweat and semen a nostalgia for hedonistic days gone by.

The nature of the epidemic made us realize that the learning of these elders disappeared with their dying bodies. We were losing precious repositories of knowledge as the epidemic culled an entire generation. A tenuous chain of knowledge, the shamanic tradition of passing cultural wisdom from one generation to another was broken. AIDS not only ravaged the bodies of individuals and their friends and lovers, it created a cultural vacuum, disrupting conduits of knowledge from one generation to the next. It left huge physical and cultural gaps that could never be replaced.

In the early days of the epidemic there were whispers about those who disappeared from our lives. We all knew about someone who was sick but didn't know what was happening. It was a steep learning curve, akin to coming out all over again. Living through the epidemic, the world of unbridled desire I experienced through Vern and his friends gave way to a world of fear, restriction and loathing. The hope of youth was deferred as it disappeared among the bodies of dying young men. I walked through a carnival of death and lived through an epidemic that politicized sexuality, joy, transgression and desire, birthing acts of anger, rage, rebellion and resistance.

The deaths of so many lovers and so many friends made death familiar, a macabre companion that came too early. So many barstools remained empty, following too many funerals. So many died during this time that death became a part of our lives; we danced to the Masque of Red Death. We normalized and assimilated a disease that culled an entire generation. Vern died in 1991.

Having to accept death that came generations too early made me angry. I was angry at the disease, I was angry at death and I was angry at how society ignored the deaths of so many young men because they were queer. The anger that comes with this can be powerful, but it is also exhausting. In the face of so many deaths, of so much ignorance and inattention it's easy to become disillusioned by the inability of the world to change. My only solution at the time was to run away. To retreat from so many deaths I went back to school and then to China, as far away as I could get.

Looking back, trying to find meaning in the battles that were fought by those who had nothing to lose, we found strength in each other. Living through the epidemic we learned how powerful we are as community and how we could affect change. The battles we fought in the 1970s for acceptance, quite literally in the 1980s became a fight for our lives. In the face of the epidemic we fought for better care, for new drugs and for safe places to die. In the end we had to bring meaning to the lives we lost and to those who survived.

I thank Vern for showing me how powerful we are as a community. He taught me to celebrate queer culture and everything we bring to the world. It is too easy in a homophobic world to forget the power that comes from difference. While our desires bring us together, queer culture builds a strong bond. Queerness can shatter sexual, social, cultural and moral ideals. Vern made being queer transgressive, fun and sexy. In the face of the deaths of so many friends, he told me those who die are never really gone, as long as we tell their stories. Like the sparks of a dying fire they remain inside of each of us and every time we speak about them they come alive again. I like this idea. Telling Vern's story means he is still with us. I know him and now you do too. Like a lot of queer pioneers, his story is that of one man who tried to find himself and in the process helped a community come together.

A Wiff of the Monster:
Encounters with Scott Symons
IAN YOUNG

"I certainly am 'a legend in my own time' in Canada... I am also a Canadian of formidable cultural background and education. And eloquent." —Scott Symons

"He was a catalyst for changing the fabric of society. He tells the truth." —Donald Martin

"A negative catalyst going through life on autopilot." —Dennis Lee

"A genius without talent." —John Robert Colombo

"I'll be the organ grinder and you can be the monkeys." —Scott Symons

"That's a hell of a letter to send to me!"

The loud voice over the phone—angry, male, tremolo—had woken me from an afternoon nap, and whoever it was had not announced himself. As I mumbled "Who's this?" into the receiver, I realized the caller was—had to be—Scott Symons, thirty-eight-year-old *enfant terrible* of the Toronto literary scene circa 1971. He was shouting at me from the Bracebridge monastery to which he habitually retreated. I had written Scott a letter he didn't like. And now there would be a price to pay because as Scott said—and this was not the only time he is reported to have said it—"no one fucks with Scott Symons and gets away with it!"

I had met Scott Symons four years earlier when a mutual interest in Allen Ginsberg brought us both to Toronto's Convocation Hall in 1967, the year of the nation's Centennial and the legendary Summer of Love. Canada's 100th year as a nation had a particularly liberating effect on the young, who experienced it as not only a watershed in the country's history and outlook, but as a long-awaited national coming of age, the occasion marked by Expo 67, an extravagant World's Fair in Montreal.

A cultural breakthrough began in the early sixties with the emergence of a new crop of artists, writers and publishing houses, coincided with the rise of the hippie movement and the emergence of a national leader of a new sort—Pierre Elliott Trudeau. By 1967, Canada's Flower Children were being uprooted, shaken loose and scattered across the nation, and the streets and cafés of Toronto's Yorkville bohemia had become fertile ground for artists and restive youth from across the country. I was a twenty-two-year-old college student with a handful of verses published in two little magazines. One was called *One*; it was a discreet, rather obscure American periodical for homosexuals. The other was the once-staid Victoria College literary journal *Acta Victoriana*. *Acta* was published from a one-room cellar with an inconspicuous entrance half-hidden by a well-manicured lawn. It was a cut above the average college lit mag, being both attractive and readable. The student staff were an astonishingly talented—and handsome—lot and included three future Governor General's Award winners: David

Gilmour, Greg Hollingshead and John Ayre, future biographer of Vic's preeminent intellectual Northrop Frye. Next door at the theatre space, Ayre's playwright friend Graham Jackson was causing a frisson of excitement. With his luminous eyes, luxuriant curls and a slight limp that gave him a Byronic swagger, Graham turned heads just by entering a room.

While the student writers edited *Acta*, Vic's faculty included Frye himself and poets Dennis Lee, David Knight, Francis Sparshott and Frye's disciple and rumoured paramour (there were whispers of a secret passage behind the bookshelves), the imperious Jay MacPherson. In her quarters, Dr. MacPherson presided over her own chilly poetry salon, dispensing literary formulae like castor oil.

The poems I published at Vic seem unexceptional now but struck Canadian readers of the day as unusually daring. With titles like "The Moth Boy" and "The Skull," they were openly gay in a way that had never been seen in CanLit. In high school I had explored books of a certain tendency, from Plato to Stephen Spender, but in the sixties, same-sex relationships were just beginning to peek out of the Canadian literary closet. An early breakthrough had come in 1964 when the British house of Secker & Warburg published *The Desert of the Heart*, a novel by the American-born Jane Rule. The first home-grown products came the following year. Edward Lacey's mordant poetry chapbook, *The Forms of Loss,* became the first openly gay book published in Canada. And John Herbert's riveting prison drama *Fortune and Men's Eyes* was workshopped at Stratford. Considered far too shocking for Canadians, it failed to find a sponsor until 1967 when it opened off-Broadway and became an instant hit.

The year before, the much-anticipated Centennial saw the appearance of a brilliant second novel by Leonard Cohen, anointed disciple of the messianic Irving Layton, the man who brought sex to Canada. *Beautiful Losers* had an important gay character, the mysterious soap-collecting separatist referred to only as F, a "hopped-up" radical who dies "in a padded cell, his brain rotted from too much dirty sex." No role models here, but the sixties were nevertheless bringing rapid changes to Canada. By 1967, the country Frederick Philip Grove thirty years before had called "a non-conductor for any sort of intellectual current" was suddenly effecting cultural electricity. As one observer put it, "everyone's sexuality was bouncing off the walls." Even so, Toronto the Good was not ready for the explosive *succès de scandale* that followed.

Combat Journal for Place d'Armes: A Personal Narrative was released by Canada's leading publishing house McClelland & Stewart at the beginning of 1967 as its author's Centennial gift to the nation. It was in no way a conventional novel, in that it reclaimed the original meaning of the word novel—new. This was something new. The authentic, insistent voice of a delirious Tory renegade who can't stop writing diaries. The "personal narrative" of *Place d'Armes* is an oddly complex journalistic montage. The original hardcover version was ingeniously designed by master printer Stan Bevington to resemble an old-fashioned notebook, complete with attached prints, postcards and fold-out maps—a time-travelling jacket, with big pockets.

Place d'Armes relates the story of a married, well-connected Torontonian named Hugh Anderson, whose life parallels that of his creator. Anderson, an authoritarian elitist in a love-hate relationship with his own class, country and background, rages against a Canadian culture he sees as denying both its British roots and its capacity for sensuous, and sensual, self-expression. Anderson is an avid hater whose targets range from Methodism and William Lyon Mackenzie to the new flag, Expo 67 and various passersby on the street whose aesthetic sensibilities he longs to whip—literally—into shape.

Hugh Anderson's escape from an emasculated culture he blames for having blocked, perhaps blighted, his power to love involves immersing himself in the life of Montreal's historic Place d'Armes, and having sex with the young hustlers he meets there who "touch him in a way no one has ever touched him in his own community," presumably because he never made it down Yonge Street as far as the St. Charles Tavern. While recording this pilgrimage in his diary, Anderson is also at work on a novel about a character called Alexander, who is yet another authorial double. Or triple. Unusually for so personal a novelist, Symons writes always in the third person. His fictionalized journals involve a series of near-identical alter egos, each furiously writing about the next. One of them has a Governor General's Award.

A brief excerpt from *Combat Journal for Place d'Armes*:

> The gift of insite. That is my battle in La Place. The right to remain open... to see... to have insite. I must incite insite. And if it is necessary to incite homosexation to propitiate my long rejected insite, then it must be done. ... If I cannot, then I am dead. But if I do I risk my sanity!...
>
> Only this diary keeps me firmly in 3-D... when I am in flight from the disembodiment of 2-D or in pursuit of 4-D... 4-D—my unknown birthright, constrained into 3-D, and finally dissolved by 2-D (the proxy plenitude of the positivist priests... professorial, psychiatrical, professions).
>
> It involves three different men, moralities, societies... visions. Each in irreparable conflict.
>
> In 4-D body is imbedded... a world of love.
>
> In 3-D body is detached... world of common-sense.
>
> In 2-D body is dissolved... world of non-sense.

> And the Canadian is exposed in a unique imme-
> diacy to all three at once. His American heritage is
> 2-D (the American dream); his British heritage is 3-D
> (Parliamentarian's Club); his French-Catholic heritage is
> 4-D (Peasant Baroque!)....
>
> I become either Protean, or insane!

Though the "Personal Narrative" of *Place d'Armes* does include the tangled thread of a plot, its strength is in its spirited, all-out manhandling of the language. Rendered in five different typefaces, it is both playful and enraged (or self-indulgent, depending on your point of view), often overwrought, and sprinkled with odd barbarisms ("psychiat-rical," "parasite" as a verb), useful coinages ("homosentient") and delicious McLuhanish puns like "the hermaphrobike," who could well be a relative of the suicidal Danish Vibrator in Cohen's *Beautiful Losers*. Its trajectory (Scott's language, I mean, not the Danish Vibrator, who merely threw him-self into the sea) occasionally soars heroically, only to turn abruptly on itself for yet another vitriolic but pointless—because endlessly repeated—confrontation with Canada, and with the reader. "Exposé 67."

The book is full of abusive tantrums; as Mencken sagely observed, "the public likes to read abuse." Symons harangues the reader in a fictional language suggestive of a series of experimental, sometimes discordant jazz riffs, many of which elide and mutate and instead of resolving, feverishly repeat, eventually disintegrating, or collapsing into them-selves. The voice is strictly solo, but we are treated to some dazzling and spirited improvisations throughout the gig. It is Scott Symons'—and Hugh Anderson's—wild verbal probes that provide inspired comic relief to Place d'Armes, without which it would be intolerable, and probably unreadable.

Scott Symons and his protagonist were not the first Anglo-Saxons to slough off their past, heal their psychic wounds and warm their cockles by consorting with prostitutes in less Protestant climes. But Symons, award-winning journalist, Rosedale elitist, scion of the establishment, delivered his message from the sexual—and political—front lines in nearby French Canada. It was brave, personal, "homosentient," and enormously angry, and English Canada was quite shaken by it. The fact that Symons was no stray dog but "the pedigreed son of a Rosedale bitch" made his barking-mad dash for freedom all the more unlikely, and unseemly. And shocking.

The dichotomy between Scott's attitude and his background—and his ambivalence about both—were highlighted by the pair of contrasting author's photos on the paperback edition of *Place d'Armes*. On the front cover Scott is dressed with casual ease in a duffle-coat and sneakers. On the back, a formal portrait by Ashley and Crippen has him brooding with hand on brow, wearing a cravat. These images were reflected by two matching, or rather unmatching, descriptive blurbs, one printed above the other. The first could only have been written by Scott, or someone channelling him: it emphasizes the Combat Journal as an all-out "assault" on its "target"—an urban environment in which nothing is what it purports to be. It concludes:

> As (Hugh Anderson) discovers that these buildings are people, places, himself, multidimensioned, he loses his mind, becomes a figment of the imagination of La Place d'Armes, keeps encountering predatorial denizens, Blondebeestes, Royal Canadian Commissars, is saved only by an enactment which destroys his male maidenhead forever and relentlessly resurrected arraigns all Montreal

before him—whip-bitch, federaste [Federaste or féderaste, a conflation of "federaliste" and "péderaste," was a coinage of Quebec separatists alluding to the alleged sexual proclivities of their federalist opponents, particularly Pierre Elliott Trudeau.], Exposé 67— invulnerable accusation, then turns and plunges into La Place to complete his mission by giving Body and Blood.

Whew! And that was just the blurb!

This was Symons in full bandolier-bedecked combat fatigues. And there was more to come. Underneath, prominently placed but in smaller type, was set out a different set of credentials. A sober recital that could have been cribbed from Who's Who paraded the insurgent's august ancestors, his degrees from Cambridge and the Sorbonne, his National Newspaper Award, his prestigious curatorial positions, his visiting professorship, his consultancy at the Smithsonian. Curiously, no mention of that old standby of the respectable author: the wife. But clearly, Scott Symons wanted it known that he was not just any old rebel off the street, or la Place. He was *somebody*.

Specifically, he was the maternal grandson of the legendary William Perkins Bull, the wealthy Toronto eccentric known as "the Duke of Rosedale." Bull, an oil and lumber baron, was an historian, naturalist and philanthropist, advisor to Prime Ministers Laurier and Borden, prominent Freemason, and personal attorney of department store magnate Timothy Eaton. He published an array of books said to have been written largely by his stable of researchers. His daughter, Scott's mother, was known in Rosedale as "the Pink Lady," not for her politics which were quite conventional, but for the powerful cocktails she served her guests.

Despite his establishment background, Symons proclaimed, "My heart is Quebecois!" Yet his novelistic view of his Montreal sexual experiences is as deeply ambiguous as the rest of his feelings. Hugh Anderson is seen as "hellbent for heaven...sainting for sinhood....To see La Place, to write my novel, to come alive, again, I must fall, utterly. To share my love, I must humiliate me... must grovel. Stand waist deep in the shit... and then sing." This tormented view of sex, sin and sanctity is more Baudelaire/Genet than Whitman/Carpenter. The English poet Kenneth Hopkins quipped that Scott was "waist deep in the shit, crying Shit!"

Combat Journal for Place d'Armes records a series of encounters that often seem more martial, or more ceremonial, than amatory. The metaphor of the War of the Sexes is a common, indeed ancient one in heterosexual lore, but is surprisingly rare in gay discourse; there are almost no fights in gay bars. But *Place d'Armes* was precursor to a number of works published during the Gay Liberation period of the seventies. *The Wild Boys*, William Burroughs' paean to post-pubescent anarchy, appeared in 1971, and John Rechy's *The Sexual Outlaw* in 1977. The young men in *The Wild Boys* are runaways and castaways who employ bizarre weapons and whom society tries, and fails, to destroy; the young men in *The Sexual Outlaw* are depicted as urban front-line fighters, shock troops, in a sexual guerrilla war against their own society. Their bodies are their weapons. The New York gay writer George Whitmore suggested the point of engaging in extreme sex was to be seen to do it "without flinching," i.e. sex as defiance, a courageous proof of one's masculinity.

Whitmore's colleague Edmund White suggested that gay men should regard their venereal diseases as badges of honour, like combat medals in a revolutionary sexual war. *Place d'Armes* presented the first of a rising generation not of activists necessarily, but of combative sexual outlaws. What gave rise to them? John Rechy answered with one word: "Rage."

At any rate, it seems evident the outraged, enraged and outrageous chief combat journalist of Place d'Armes may well be suffering from acute battle fatigue, not to say shell shock. He seems a man in precarious psychological equilibrium, perhaps in imminent danger of mental collapse. How the author is doing is less certain.

Canadian reviewers recognized the novel's crotchety uniqueness, some taking a not unsympathetic view of its challenge to frosty, thawing Upper Canadian puritanism. But one particular review was to become notorious, and to help make Scott notorious: Robert Fulford's column in the *Toronto Star* was titled (presumably by a sub-editor) "A monster from Toronto." It was judicious, insightful, and so devastating that Scott was still smarting from it more than three decades later and an ocean away.

Fulford's piece began: "The hero of Scott Symons' first novel, *Place d'Armes* may well be the most repellent single figure in the recent history of Canadian writing." Fulford describes Hugh Anderson as "a monster of snobbishness still wedded to an aesthetic view of life that can be called—depending on the degree of your benevolence—either aristocratic or fascist." Symons, Fulford explains, is "writing a novel about a man who is writing a novel about a man who is writing a novel," each of the novelists being more like Symons than the last. "This is nothing if not ingenious, and it works, but halfway through the book it grows tiresome."

The column went on to describe the book as overwritten as well as overproduced, revealing "more ambition than talent....The author makes each of his points half a dozen times, and they do not improve through repetition." *Place d'Armes* was characterized as "a kind of higher journalism," (this was the heyday of Tom Wolfe and Hunter Thompson). "When it departs from this,—when it tries to develop human insights, or tries to convey passion—it fails badly. The hero's problem is that he cannot love; the author's problem is that he can write neither with nor about love."

Symons'—and much of the reading public's—reaction to the *Star's* review focused on its title. It was the fictional Hugh Anderson, of course, not his creator, who had been accused specifically of loveless monstrosity. But the title stuck. The Monster from Toronto was born. Symons was understandably upset, forgetting in his anger that 1) "All publicity is good publicity," and 2) "If you dish it out, you should be able to take it."

Fulford's column was hardly the first time a Canadian author had been subjected to a journalistic savaging of his or her fictional creation. Three years previously, George Robertson had written in the pages of Canadian Literature that the central character of Margaret Laurence's now-classic *The Stone Angel*, was "as unpleasant a heroine as one is likely to meet... proud, bitter, and vengeful... bloated... blind and selfish." (George Robertson, "An Artist's Progress," *Canadian Literature* No. 21, Summer 1964.) Apparently no umbrage was taken on that occasion as Mrs. Laurence did not assume the characterization was necessarily aimed at her. Symons felt no such distance from his fictional clones. Thus Fulford's verdict was understandably viewed as an unwarranted personal denunciation.

When I first met Scott, the furor over his debut novel was still breaking. *Place d'Armes* had been published in January. In February, the University College Literary & Athletic Society at the University of Toronto sponsored a controversial "psychedelic festival" called Perception '67.

This encompassed a variety of events including a series of visionary (or disorienting) "Mind Excursion Rooms" and a Saturday night "Happening" at Convocation Hall featuring the music group The Fugs and, as an opening act, Beat poet Allen Ginsberg, who read poems and chanted Buddhist hymns. Psychedelic guru Dr. Timothy Leary had also been invited but the federal government had barred him from entering the country, citing a conviction for "drug trafficking" (i.e. transporting marijuana across state lines). At the last minute, the University College Principal, Douglas LePan, announced a strict ban from all college properties of "users or advocates of the drug LSD." "Recently," Principal LePan explained, "a far from negligible number of our students had psychic breakdowns and had to withdraw and enter psychiatric wards." Faced with such disturbing phenomena, LePan's administrative instinct was to suppress, not encourage, discussion. LePan, an author and former diplomat, had been an aide to Lester Pearson. His war novel *The Deserter* scandalously won the 1964 Governor General's Award over *The Stone Angel*. (LePan's fear of bad publicity was seen in a new light when he came out of the closet in 1990 at the age of seventy-six.)

Even without Leary or an official panel on drugs, the mid-winter Happening was a success, with a number of Toronto luminaries in attendance, including Marshall McLuhan sporting a "third eye" in the form of a light-refracting disc strapped to his forehead. I didn't see McLuhan but while engrossed in listening to Ginsberg, I became aware that the man I was staring at, sitting directly across the aisle from me, was someone I recognized as the author of a novel I had just read. I had picked up a copy of *Combat Journal for Place d'Armes* soon after it appeared, and admired its inventive language and unprecedented audacity. After the reading, I introduced myself, had a brief conversation with the author, and wandered off home to think about Ginsberg and Symons. Soon afterwards, Scott left the country in an exodus that was to become notorious.

Before *Place d'Armes* changed everything, Scott Symons was known in both English and French Canada as a prescient, award-winning journalist. His series—in French—forecasting the Quiet Revolution had won the National Newspaper Award. He was a respectably married man with close ties to the academic world, a pious Anglican who retreated from time to time to a provincial monastery to engage in fervent prayer. Those who knew him on a personal level frequently found him sharp, abrasive, and unpredictable—decidedly not a gentleman or what passed for gentleman among those Scott called (reverently, in a chat with the Queen Mother) "Your Majesty's Royal Americans." He was still a celebrated and eminently respectable figure when he received an invitation to speak to the students of a small private school near Bracebridge, Ontario. It was there that he met the strikingly handsome, seventeen-year-old John McConnell, the bright, alienated son of a prominent Toronto banker. This was the beginning of the odyssey frequently described since as "running away to Mexico with a teenage boy"—a notorious tandem flight that in fact never occurred. Later conversations with both Scott and John gave a more accurate, though no less extraordinary, story.

Scott was born on July 13, 1933. After graduating from Trinity College at the University of Toronto, he won a Commonwealth Fellowship to King's College, Cambridge. From there he went to the Sorbonne. The woman he married at the age of twenty-five was, he often reminded people, the granddaughter of a leading bank president. The marriage had gotten off to a rocky start when Scott's rudely provocative speech disrupted his own wedding, but it lasted for ten years and produced a son, born in Paris while Scott was working in the wine trade.

"So you could have been a French vintner, Scott," I once remarked.

"Maybe I should have been. But while I was in France I met Julien Green."

Julien Green was an American-born writer who lived in France and wrote in French. It was over dinner with Green and his younger lover (whom he later adopted) novelist Eric Jourdan, that Scott's closet doors first became seriously unhinged. Green, as Scott put it, "introduced me to my gay factor"—not through any erotic suggestion but simply by his eyes going "right through me." Photos of Green show him as an attractive man with a good-humoured smile. But Scott experienced Green's gaze rather as E.M. Forster experienced a friendly pat on the bum delivered by the openly gay George Merrill at the cottage he shared with Whitman's disciple Edward Carpenter. "It seemed to go straight through the small of my back into my ideas," Forster recalled, "without involving any thought." The frisson from that touch was the genesis of Forster's classic gay novel *Maurice*.

Julien Green's searching gaze apparently opened up long dormant feelings in Scott. According to Charles Taylor's masterly essay in *Six Journeys: A Canadian Pattern*, Scott, while a young student at Trinity College Schools in Port Hope, had contracted an affair with another boy-an affair that Scott broke off when, believing that "his body and his desires were dirty," he "felt an overwhelming inner veto." Later, Taylor wrote, "he would blame the school, his family and his society for compelling him to suppress his love." Scott apparently came to see this repudiation as "decisive, and crippling." He remained, in his own words, an "eternal thirteen; eternally the boy reaching out to touch but never being allowed to do so... except as Mommy and Authority permitted." The penetrating look of a French novelist across a Parisian dining table had resurrected these awkward suppressed memories. Nevertheless, Scott and his young wife returned to Canada to live at her wealthy family's Ontario farm, which they purchased with money from Symons' family. And Scott wrote his acclaimed series of articles for *La Presse* on the coming political and social upheaval in Quebec.

"I was saying that Canada was going to explode," Scott told me. "There was going to be a revolution. Trudeau and I became good friends through that. He was editing *Cité Libre* at the time.... We had a real symbiotic relationship that we were both aware had a sexual component. We were both aware that the other was homosentient. In those days, no one said anything about homosexuality. Many of the guys at *La Presse* were gay but you certainly didn't walk up to them and announce it. Of course I was married at the time."

Scott's establishment connections and a wide and discerning knowledge of Canadian antiques paved the way for him to become Curator of Canadiana at Toronto's Royal Ontario Museum, one of a number of positions from which he was dismissed for causing too many problems. About the same time, he told his wife about his growing attraction to men. "She said if you want to do that, you should do it." So he left her in Ontario and headed for Montreal.

Those trips, and his voluminous journals, were, Scott said, his way of knowing himself and expressing himself. "Because you couldn't talk about anything in my culture in those days. You couldn't even talk about heterosexuality. Though the French Canadians were quite a bit looser than we were. But you couldn't announce that you were into cocksucking. It would have ended everything. But I published

Place d'Armes as my gift to Canada for the Centennial. And that led to the breakup of my marriage. We had no intention of separating. We adored each other," he insisted. "But her parents were so nosey and determined to run her life. Her mother was noted for being a cruel woman."

I reminded him that he had been having an affair with the young John McConnell. He recalled meeting John at Muskoka Lakes College, a private school "for kids whose parents couldn't figure out what to do with them. They were a wealthy family. His father ran (Ontario Premier) John Robarts' ad campaigns. I was on a retreat at the monastery in Bracebridge and was invited to give a talk at the school. After the talk, there was this beautiful boy with flaming red hair, standing in the hall, waiting for me."

Though only seventeen at the time, John was tall and well-built and looked like a lumberjack, which he later briefly became.

"What did you say to him?" I asked.

"Every instinct told me he was profound trouble. I said 'I don't want to talk to you.'"

Scott's answer surprised me. I too had met a beautiful, extraordinary seventeen-year-old—in a Yorkville sidewalk café—and had fallen in love with him. Law or no law, it would never have occurred to me to tell Richard Phelan "I don't want to talk to you." Scott had evidently been conflicted in ways that were foreign to me. But teenage boys can be wilful, and John was not about to be brushed off so easily.

"He had set his sights on me," said Scott, "and he was going to get me. But his parents sent him to a gilded cage in Nassau. I went to San Miguel de Allende in Mexico where I was hanging out with a group of painters including York Wilson and Leonard Brooks. He got a message to me. And I sent him a telegram saying 'Take up your

cock and walk.' I remember sitting in the courtyard garden and there he was."

John later confirmed Scott's recollection. So, all later
sensational accounts to the contrary, Scott Symons never
did "run away to Mexico with a seventeen-year-old."
Nonetheless, John's well-connected father set the police of
three countries on the pair, posting a hefty reward for their
arrest. When John heard about this, he contacted his sister,
asking her to warn their parents that he would kill himself if
Scott was jailed. Word soon came back that the reward had
been rescinded and that John could pick up his passport at
the Canadian embassy. The couple then re-entered Canada
and fled "to grizzly country" on the Northern BC coast.
After various adventures and misadventures there, including
a stint at lumberjacking, they resurfaced in Toronto in 1970,
where I ran into Scott again.

In the previous year, my long-standing efforts to start a gay
organization at the University of Toronto had finally paid off.
Whereas before, no-one had dared to come out of the closet,
now in the wake of the Stonewall riots in New York and the
Trudeau-sponsored decriminalization at home, the situation
had suddenly changed. In November of 1969, the first official
meeting of the University of Toronto Homophile Association
launched what would become the Canadian Gay Liberation
movement. When I learned that Canada's best-known gay
author was back in town and staying at the Norman Elder
Museum and Gallery in Yorkville, I lost no time in dropping
by to ask him to speak to the new group.

By then, Scott's wife, considering herself abandoned,
had divorced him, forbidden him ever to see his son again,
and sold his property at auction. When I commiserated
with Scott about his divorce, he placed the blame squarely
upon his in-laws, seeing them as representing an implacably

hostile Rosedale establishment of bland, powerful eunuchs and their cruel, unavailable wives. The fact that he had left his wife to live in distant parts with a teenaged lover did not seem to Scott to be grounds for divorce. "The vile cow, doesn't she know how much I love her?"

By my next encounter with Scott, both of us had new books making their way to the store shelves. My poems in *Acta* had been spotted by Dennis Lee, who was about to launch a new publishing company, House of Anansi, with the novelist Dave Godfrey. Dennis asked me for a manuscript, and Anansi published *Year of the Quiet Sun* late in 1969. About the same time, Scott published his second book, an extraordinary production originally called *The Smugly Fucklings*, but after much persuasion released under the more sober title of *Civic Square*.

At 848 pages, *Civic Square: An Original Manuscript* by Scott Symons made *Combat Journal for Place d'Armes* seem concise and coherent. Neither Scott nor his publisher Jack McClelland had relished the daunting task of cutting the idiosyncratic— and ever-expanding—manuscript, and it was recognized that, uncut, it would be, as editor John Robert Colombo later put it, "unmarketable." Scott gave his publishers the same permission he gave the surgeon who circumcised his son: "Just take a little bit." The work was eventually issued in a small edition as a gestetnered typescript of unbound sheets stacked in a large, powder-blue box that simulated the trademark "Birks boxes" of the fashionable Toronto retailers. Each copy of the book was personalized by Scott with distinctive coloured glyphs of fiery, flaming phalli. It remains a controversial work to this day, having been judged (by Patrick Watson) as "extremely skilful" and (by Dennis Lee) as "very badly written."

When I arrived at Norm Elder's Yorkville home and private museum, Scott was sitting on the single bed in his room. He made a gentlemanly pass at me, which I deflected. Scott concluded I must find him "intimidating;" as it happened, I just didn't fancy him. When I moved the conversation to the subject of speaking engagements, Scott said he would be happy to speak to the UTHA and a date was set. We chatted a little about his background, his and his wife's ancestors, and his boyhood at Trinity College Schools, which, knowing my English background, he informed me was "the Canadian Eton."

"I went to Beal," I said, with a certain emphasis. Scott looked at me in silence. Obviously he had never heard of Beal, which was not surprising as it was an undistinguished Ilford grammar school. He shifted his buttocks and emitted a loud and pungent fart and we sat silently, savouring the moment. Scott seemed quite at ease in Norman's quarters, though he later confided that he "didn't sleep comfortably" there because of the pet boa constrictors Norm kept down the hall.

Another young writer who visited Scott around that time was the Lancashire poet Michael Higgins, who was then living in Toronto. When he dropped in on Scott's rooms, Michael was carrying a guidebook to the city of York which he showed Scott, seeing it as an alien but comparable locale to the *Place d'Armes*. "He snarled with contempt," Michael recalled, "and (literally) threw the book at me, hitting my arm, and saying something along the lines of 'I've been there before, one doesn't need this!'" Michael left thinking Scott to be uncouth as well as overrated. He never finished reading *Place d'Armes*.

Other meetings were more successful. Scott enjoyed brief liaisons with several UTHA members. The young gay activist Michael Pearl told Scott, after an erotic encounter, "You're a cute old number!" Scott met more formally with our little gay organization more than once in the months that followed, sometimes accompanied by John McConnell. He spoke about their relationship, and about modern civilization's rising competence and declining compassion. He felt Canada was an anaphrodisiac society with a crippling fear of tenderness. He found at the UTHA "a level of intimacy and honesty in discussion," but felt that more should be said about "the nature of a good and deep and extended relationship between two guys—all the difficulties of being a homosentient person in this society." He told the group how both he and John had come from wealthy Toronto homes and, "desperate for love and affection, had to knock down just about every barrier that exists in the Protestant society book to reach out and touch each other." A favourite topic was "the amount of hate" existing not only in society in general but specifically in "the failure to touch" existing in the middle class marriage: what he called "the hate space."

Scott celebrated "the guerrilla warfare of the new sensibility," comparing himself to Che Guevara, an insurgent bedecked with explosives. He found much to enjoy in the emerging gay world, but was shocked by the amount of hate he found there. What the gay world had not done successfully, he felt, was putting men "in touch with each other on a long-term basis very intimately, very relaxedly." He found—and I saw this as quite perceptive—that in both heterosexual and homosexual relationships, "you (often) turn onto somebody, and then when he or she gets close to you, cut him or her off. That was the control system." Scott called this "the negative orgasm cycle." He and John, he told us, were trying to overcome this unhappy situation, and it was "a long, hard trip… the big battle. And it's a battle the whole of our society is in."

By that point, Scott and John had spent some time living in a remote part of Newfoundland, thanks to the first of a series of cash subsidies organized by Scott's friend and patron Charles Taylor, writer son of the millionaire horse breeder E.P. Taylor. (At one UTHA get-together Scott had proudly displayed on a tabletop a small stack of high-denomination banknotes, spread into a fan like a hand of playing cards.) The couple had been welcomed by the rural islanders and the motherly Ma Snook. Scott came to admire the locals' "quick responses" and "eyes that look straight into you, as if probing your beauty... constantly alert and aware... fresh and clean inside themselves, like the sea on a calm sunny day." And, he found, they were men and women "honest about their sex. There is none of the morbid division between their desires and their values... so true on the mainland.... They celebrate in their flesh, and it is beautiful." Nevertheless, at least one woman-friend there was offended at what she presumed was Scott's "seduction of a gracious, inexperienced young boy." In fact, John had been sexually active with men for over a year prior to their meeting and had been earnestly looking for an older male partner.

At the UTHA, Scott and John both spoke eloquently, and Scott quickly began to attract a personal following from among the (mostly male) members. He readily agreed to be a speaker at one of the series of public lectures the Association was sponsoring on campus. So it was that on March 25, 1971, in the university's Medical Auditorium, Scott gave a presentation advertised under the title "Canada, Orgasm and Us."

The lecture drew a considerable crowd. Scott talked of his stay in "a falling down goat house about a hundred miles up the coast" from Vancouver, and his life in Newfoundland, "tougher in its climate... it has the wonderful addition of a people and a culture four centuries old." He delighted the audience by declaiming the "Cocks are beautiful.... Cocks are Holy Rood" passage from the beginning of *Civic Square*. At one point, departing from his scripted remarks, he began to read a love letter, apparently delivered that very morning from John, who was still back in Trout River, Newfoundland. Scott then removed from the same envelope a nude photo of John which he held aloft and proceeded to circulate around the auditorium. As the lecture continued, the picture of the handsome, naked young man was passed, somewhat nervously, from hand to hand. I was sitting towards the front of the auditorium, on the aisle, and eventually the photo reached me, slightly soiled from having been dropped on the floor. The seats in front of me were empty, everyone was paying attention to Scott, and seeing no outstretched hand, I pocketed the photo to return it after the lecture. As it happened, Scott left quickly with a sizable entourage before I could reach him.

Though radical in some things, I was conservative in others. I had enjoyed hearing of Allen Ginsberg's public disrobings (on being asked "What do you mean by naked?" he had taken his clothes off to demonstrate) but it seemed to me that nude photographs of one's lover should be for private viewing or shared with a few close friends. Passing them through hundreds of sweaty fingers in a public stadium did not strike me as a great idea; displaying one's own nakedness in public is one thing, displaying someone else's, a quite different matter. I doubted it would help Scott's reputation, and if he was going to be the mutinous messiah of the new Canadian gay movement, as was beginning to appear likely, I felt there might well be dangers ahead if he didn't rethink this particular tactic.

As Scott had left for his monastery the morning after the lecture, I wrote him a brief letter suggesting he might want to rethink his approach. Before mailing the note, I thought

I should seek a second opinion. I showed it to Paul Pearce, a level-headed member of the UTHA whose judgement I trusted. As he was equally skeptical of Scott's public manner, the letter went in the post the next day, with John's photo enclosed. A couple of days later, I awoke to Scott's challenging voice from the cloister.

One of the duties and prerogatives of friendship is surely to warn of possible dangers ahead, to restrain, to urge caution and reflection. Just in case. This can cause problems, and Scott was not the first, or the last, acquaintance to excommunicate me. My letter on that occasion, if not impertinent, was certainly presumptuous, in that it was a letter that only a friend should write. I had presumed friendship where none really existed, and my little message must have sounded self-righteous, censorious, annoying. As his reaction to the *Star's* review had shown, Scott was easily rattled when not taken at his own valuation.

By this point, Richard Phelan, the schoolboy I had met during the Summer of Love four years earlier was now a world-travelling student of Buddhism. He had returned to Toronto for a stretch and he and I were hanging out together, collaborating on a book to be illustrated with his drawings. Richard had met both Scott and John and though he may not have been at the "Orgasm" lecture, he certainly had heard about it. Richard was one of those people who never speak ill of anyone, and his only remark on the lecture was "There's a difference between a ballet and a striptease!" But he could tell that Scott's phone call had upset me more than I let on, and once Scott was back in town from his retreat, Rick arranged to visit Scott to see if he could smooth things over.

According to Rick, Scott had been in no mood for tea and tête-à-tête, pressing instead for a more carnal engagement,

"All he wanted to do was have sex with me," Richard said with a shrug and a smile. When he demurred, he was accused of having "forgotten how to celebrate," which was Scott's word for fuck. "You've been in the city too long!" Scott scolded, unaware of Rick's recent wanderings in the far-flung holy places. Realizing his cause was hopeless, Richard gracefully retreated. And that was that. Scott seems never again to have talked to a gay group or associated himself with a gay cause. His brief career as a public spokesman for Gay Lib was over. The next time Scott and I spoke, well over thirty years had passed, Richard was dead, and Scott had returned from his long, self-imposed exile for the last time.

John left Scott in the summer of 1972, shortly after the publication of *Heritage,* Scott's learned, idiosyncratic "furniture novel" (*Heritage: A Romantic Look at Early Canadian Furniture*, McClelland & Stewart, 1971). "We were in a sixteen-foot trailer near Trout River Pond," he told me years later. John, who had dropped out of Grade Twelve, had expressed his desire to get a university education. "Working in lumber camps and fisheries was fine for my youth but wouldn't work for me as I aged. I needed to go back and complete my schooling and Scott could not abide that. He wanted me forever young and all for himself—including all of my future." Also complicating things was John's growing interest in homoerotic sadomasochism. John's interests, both erotic and educational, Scott interpreted as rejection, and he responded with a series of verbal assaults.

"When I told Scott I was going to leave him," John wrote, "he exploded into a rant and wouldn't calm down. I told him I was going for a walk." Scott followed John along the lakefront, tackled him, and attacked him, leaving him with a black eye. At that point, John realized he wanted to leave Scott but feared that "if I didn't hold open the possibility of living together he would become violent again." With talk of a trial separation, Scott left for Mexico, and the prospect of renewing his relationship with a woman both he and John had been involved with on a previous trip. "When Scott arrived in Mexico he found that the woman had already moved in with another man. That stirred him to make overtures about getting back together with me."

Scott attributed John's diminishing erotic interest to the pernicious influence of the "squares and smuglies," John told me. "Nothing to do with his big belly." John also began expressing an interest in exploring heterosexual relationships, partly as a way of blocking the possibility of Scott's return. "I wanted to distance myself from him far enough," he recalled, "to make impossible the resumption of our erotic relationship. Going straight served that function." Scott, of course, saw the breakup in a different light, claiming that John had been attempting to kill him by murdering their love. He interpreted John's interests not as the natural feelings and ambitions of an intelligent young man but instead as treachery and attempted homicide. He was persuaded to see a psychiatrist, who told him John was trying to exorcise his own demons (as it were) by projecting them onto Scott. In willing Scott's death, he was absolving himself of the need to commit suicide; he had been exercising a kind of "psychic voodoo." Scott's journals of this period contain many mentions of psychic voodoo, black magic and sadomasochism. He was deeply troubled about his future—and his reputation. "I can't stop him," he wrote in his journal. "And a whole nation will applaud his honesty, his decency, and pay him well…."

After his split with Scott, I continued to see John from time to time until he graduated and left the country. I remember visiting him in his small, cozy apartment near High Park when he was a university student. He told me

Scott had sometimes come to see him. On one occasion, after Scott had left, John noticed he had lifted a stack of photos of their time together. Recalling their final meeting, John remembered Scott had showed up "in full leather regalia, harness, boots, leather jacket and Master's cap." They talked briefly and were soon in bed together. Scott took his belt to John. Then, with John still naked on the bed, "Scott abruptly buckled up, suddenly exiting and leaving the apartment door wide open, screaming 'Evil! Evil! Evil!' as he strode down the hall." John never saw Scott again. He started a new life in California, where he became a therapist and a prominent member of the gay leather community.

Scott now saw himself as "a murdered man." By 1973, he had left Canada, recapitulating an earlier stay in Morocco by settling in a well-appointed compound in Essaouira, where he lived for most of the next three decades, leaving the hefty manuscript of his three-part novel *Helmet of Flesh* with Dennis Lee, who spent the next fourteen years shaping it into publishable form. Essaouira seems to have been a favourite spot for Canadian (and other) expatriates. Richard Phelan wrote to me from there in 1972, and in '78, Edward Lacey was arrested for smoking hash in one of the local cafés, jailed for two months, and deported to Spain, an incident Scott regretted not knowing about until much later.

In 1977, Charles Taylor published his book *Six Journeys: A Canadian Pattern*, a collection of sympathetic biographical sketches of Scott and five others who "followed a lonely path in search of a more sustaining vision than was offered by… Canadian society," exploring other cultures and "traditions which modern Canada seeks to denigrate." Taylor quotes Scott's belief that "the Canadian Identity is evil. I am dedicated to the total destruction of the Canadian state." What he anticipated as a replacement is not recorded.

That year, Scott published a lengthy article in a Canadian literary journal titled "The Canadian Bestiary: Ongoing Literary Depravity" (*West Coast Review*, Vol. 11, No. 3). It is an extended personal reaction to Marion Engel's 1976 novel *Bear*, an odd tale of an unhappy woman who, as Scott puts it, "seduces a poor, tatty bear." Scott was evidently deeply offended by Engel's mildly controversial novel, which confirmed and deepened his convictions about what he saw as the loathsome degeneration of English-Canadian culture. Writing the piece, he confided, his "two central feelings were scorn and outrage."

After a page or so of nervous clowning around, "A Canadian Bestiary" developed into a slashing verbal assault on *Bear* and its author. Feeling the book had been praised for all the wrong reasons, Scott obviously enjoyed venting his indignation. His point was not so much that *Bear* was an overpraised and pretentious book, rather that its very publication and acceptance exemplified the nation's smug, subcultural tawdriness, thus preventing the future publication of other, better books.

His swashbuckling assault having bloodied Ms. Engel and her Bear, Scott then mounted a scattershot attack on much of the rest of CanLit. By the end of his thirteen pages, he had savaged not only Ms. Engel ("common... culturally pretentious... with absolutely nothing to say") and her *Bear* ("spiritual gangrene... a Faustian compact with the Devil") but also Irving Layton ("a runt"), Robertson Davies ("Humbug!"), Mordecai Richler ("second rate"), Victor Coleman ("insidiously trivial"), Jacques Godbout ("a federaste"), literary immigrants ("born in Baghdad or Bongo Bongo") and even the Symons-friendly Coach House Press ("ghoulish... psychedelic masochismo"), not to mention his old nemesis Robert Fulford ("Bobo Fullblown").

In this extraordinary one-man uprising against CanLit, the only writers to emerge more or less unscathed are the two ageing doyennes Margaret Laurence and Marie-Claire Blais; Dennis Lee, then in the initial throes of sculpting Scott's monumental *Helmet of Flesh*; and one or two lesser-known figures who are damned with faint praise. The essay finishes with a disdainful denunciation of "the literature of depravity and psychic deprivation," and a ready prophecy that the next "with-it-lit" fad will be "sadomasochistic homosexuality!" which Symons characterizes, obscurely, as a "natural kickback."

Commissioning Scott to vent his opinions was like milking a rattlesnake; once you got his fangs in the jar, the venom just kept coming, and you were sure to have a saleable, if highly toxic, commodity. "A Canadian Bestiary" did cause a small stir. But Scott quickly returned to Essaouira, and I read nothing further by him until his *Helmet of Flesh* finally hit the shelves in 1986.

The first half of the novel is a mildly satirical, third-person narrative about a youngish Canadian—another Symons clone called York Mackenzie—who falls in with a dissolute group of travelling English expatriates in Morocco. In a vigorous extended passage at the centre of the novel, an ecstatic fire dance—"James sniffing the flames like wine... Flesh fused to flame in a single groaning dance"—culminates in what may or may not be a human sacrifice. A fever-ridden Mackenzie then recovers from his hallucinations in a private sanatorium. It becomes evident that York Mackenzie, like Hugh Anderson before him, is in a psychologically precarious state.

Unfortunately, from then on, the story rather falls apart as the author doesn't seem to know how to utilize the impact of his vivid central scene. One chapter, a flashback to his life with a lover called John in Newfoundland, is written mostly in Newfie dialect, which soon becomes annoying. At one point in the book, Mackenzie recalls being beaten up in a Yorkville alley on orders from John's relatives—an event which the real John did not remember from their time together, remarking that back-alley beatings had never been his family's style. Eventually, Mackenzie returns to Newfoundland, and to John, without much apparent enthusiasm.

Helmet of Flesh met with a varied reception. A careful blurb from Margaret Atwood described it as "significant and provocative… will be read and talked about for many years to come." So discerning a connoisseur of humour as Dr. Northrop Frye professed to find it "funny." Others were disappointed, judging it an unsuccessful amalgam of its editor's jovial Boys' Own adventure story approach and Scott's inchoate ravings. Some *Helmet* readers were surprised to see Scott's gracious acknowledgement of ongoing assistance from the Canada Council, the Toronto and Ontario Arts Councils, and an array of patrons, named and unnamed, including "businessmen and women, writers, media people, restauranteurs, civil servants and a Toronto bank" an apparent contradiction of his frequent contention that he had been generally anathematized, blackballed, driven into exile.

Over the years, curious bits of Scott Symons lore filtered back to Canada. The would-be gay messiah was now said to disdain gays, the gay movement, and even Trudeau's legalization of homosexuality. Symons claimed now to "hate Trudeau with a volcanic passion." His sexual preferences, he maintained, in a conversation with David Warren of the Ottawa Citizen, had been "a mistake" and "a red herring." What he really wanted, he said, was a "male revolution" against the "epistemological enormities" of feminism, the cruel Canadian women, with their "closed cunts."

In 1990, a Toronto magazine, *The Idler,* published two of Scott's essays. "Atwood-as-Icon" was a critique of the public reputation of Margaret Atwood. It made some telling observations, but was hampered by its author's appearing to have read only one or two of Atwood's works. "Mazo Was Murdered" was not so much a defence of the prolific, now underrated novelist Mazo de la Roche, as an attack on the detractors of her epic Jalna series and the Anglo-Canadian cultural tradition it represents. Both essays were included in Christopher Elson's compendium *Dear Reader: Selected Scott Symons,* which Gutter Press published in 1998. Shortly before the book appeared, Canadian filmmaker Nik Sheehan was putting the finishing touches on his documentary film about Scott. *God's Fool* will stand with Charles Taylor's essay as an authoritative documentation of Scott's unique personality.

One old friend interviewed in the film remembers Scott and his wife attending an art gallery function, Scott playing the part of a snake charmer, with his wife as the snake. A former student remarks, "It was very important for him to believe that he loved women." His protégé Donald Martin sees him as essentially a truth-teller, and an influential social force, while David Gilmour recalls the darker aspects of Scott's self-promotion, and remembers his own incredulous youthful reaction to the massive, uncut helmet of flesh: "Where is the valium? Oh, this *is* the Valium!"

Scott himself declares that he is a spiritual African: "I love Morocco and the Moroccans love me…*Je suis Zulu!*" he adds with a chuckle. And he supplies an entirely fictional version of his long-ago meeting with John McConnell. The school hallway in Muskoka has now become a forest through which John rides with the wind in his hair, a romantic young Tartar on a galloping horse, confronting Scott in a scene reminiscent of Marlon Brando eyeing Robert Forster in John Huston's 1967 homo-gothic *Reflections in a Golden Eye*. In Scott's recapitulation, John teasingly calls him a big, black bear—not a tame bear like Ms. Engel's mangy mascot, but a wild animal with impressive, horse-frightening power.

The Scott Symons that Nik Sheehan captures in his Moroccan redoubt appears to have lost much of his vitality, delivering many of his speeches while lying down. By the end of the film he seems bloated, desperate, and somehow unclean, his watchful eyes shifty and menacing as he wanders through his lonely compound ranting "How dare they!" to the walls, or making notebook entries in a deserted rooftop restaurant. One can't help thinking of Big Daddy's resonant line in *Cat on a Hot Tin Roof*: "There's an air of mendacity in this house!" Scott's companion of almost twenty years, Aaron Klokeid, is seen briefly, but never speaks.

Regrettably absent from the large cast of commentators in *God's Fool* is Charles Taylor, whose finances kept Scott in pocket and out of trouble for almost thirty years. In fact Taylor had been very ill, and died before the film was made. It was the unexpected demise of his true friend and patron at the age of sixty-three that brought down a slow curtain on Scott's Moroccan sojourn. Early in 2000, Nik Sheehan, now back in Canada, received two long-distance calls from Morocco. The first was from the Canadian embassy in Rabat, informing him that Scott had been instructed to leave the country within twenty-four hours. The second was from an emotionally shattered Aaron Klokeid, now apparently "abandoned to his fate."

Within a week, Scott was back in Toronto, with a colourful story to explain his sudden reversal of fortune. The mild-mannered Aaron, he confided to Nik Sheehan and others, had become "mixed up in a Thugee ritual murder cult involving international drug smugglers." Scott's personal investigations into this sinister conspiracy had so rattled the Moroccan authorities that, Scott's connections to the King notwithstanding, he had seen fit to leave, turning over his "ranch" to the local villagers as a parting gift.

The word from Morocco was somewhat different. There it was maintained that Scott had used Charles Taylor's final subsidy to have an additional turret added to the writing room of his large house. With the loss of his sole source of income, Scott's many substantial debts to local businesses soon came due, and the government, anxious to avoid further unpleasantness, had issued an expulsion order. Aaron Klokeid, left to his own devices, was apparently bailed out by his Vancouver family.

By the time Scott arrived back in his birthplace, many of the principal players from the old days had quit the scene. After many years abroad, Edward Lacey had succumbed to a heart attack in a Toronto rooming house in 1995. Michael Higgins had returned to England. Richard Phelan and Michael Pearl had both died in the pandemic that devastated the North American gay community in the eighties and nineties. By the onset of the millennium, so many of my old friends had been lost to AIDS that I was not surprised to hear that John McConnell too was now said to be "very sick."

Scott had arrived in Toronto with no money and in deteriorating health. He first sought shelter at Massey College where his old chum John Fraser was now Master, but, alas, they were "full up." After a brief stay next door at Trinity, he prevailed on a succession of friends including Nik Sheehan and crime writer James Dubro. For a while he lived unobtrusively in the basement of a fraternity house before being ejected by the authorities. From there he decamped to what Dubro described as "flea-bag rooming houses" in

Kensington Market. I caught up to him in 2001 at a literary get-together memorializing Edward Lacey. He seemed much mellowed and had apparently pardoned me for my act of *lèse-majesté* all those years before.

Scott spent his last years living at Leisure World, a crowded care home for the indigent infirm on St. George Street near the U. of T. Campus. In 2006 he shared dinner at my home in Toronto's east end, and gave what was to be his last interview. After several heart attacks and the onset of Parkinson's and diabetes, he was frail, a bit forgetful, and still eager to talk. Though much of the old bombast was gone, there were some new delusions (he believed the Prime Minister was his nephew). But he seemed a different creature from the desperate wreck captured at the end of *God's Fool*. Nicer, and more tranquil.

He reminisced about his old publisher Jack McClelland, who, he said, had considered Scott "the most important writer in his stable," but "I was kind of a peripatetic scandal and he wanted to protect himself." I asked him about his relationship with John. He had fond memories of their time in Newfoundland, and was proud that he had been asked to "give the Christmas address at the Salvation Army Church." His split with John, like his earlier split with his wife, he blamed wholly on parental malice: "They threatened to disinherit John and jail me," he said, and had hired a psychiatrist to convince John "there was nothing significant in our relationship." John's mother, he emphasized, "was a cruel woman." John, he told me, had wanted to get back together with Scott but had contracted AIDS and "died a horrible death." Aaron Klokeid, he said, had been in Morocco on his honeymoon when they met. At that encounter, Scott had apparently played the role of Julien Green but in this case, the impressionable young man did not turn away from the older expatriate writer and take his bride back to Canada but stayed with him for two decades. Eventually, he said, Aaron was "seduced by the governor's mistress."

He much enjoyed his dinner with us, was gracious to my elderly mother, and posed for a few photos in the garden. Scott seemed in his last phase to shuck off many of the psychic burdens that had made him so angry. In spite of Leisure World's painfully crowded conditions, he was cared for reasonably well there and had no problem fitting in with the other patients, who called him "the professor" (at least those who could speak). He continued to enjoy his cigarettes, and had at least one outing a week, attending regular Sunday services at St. Thomas's Anglican Church nearby. All in all, he seemed if not content, at least resigned. I never heard him complain. Perhaps all those stays in the monastery rubbed off on the old monster after all.

Not everything was sweetness and light of course. A publisher friend took him out one evening to dinner and drinks at a Bloor Street restaurant. When Pierre Trudeau's name came up in conversation, Scott grew agitated, stopping all conversation in the room and turning diners' heads by shouting "I fucked that Trudeau up the ass!"—an historic claim that, had it been true, we would surely have heard about before.

Shortly after our interview, I ran into an old Toronto friend of John's, Ian Turner, who told me Scott had been misinformed: John McConnell was in fact alive and well, and living in San Diego! I was able to contact him by email and a few days later, paid a visit to Leisure World to give Scott the good news of his ex-lover's resurrection.

John phoned Scott on Christmas Eve, 2006. Scott apparently expressed no regrets. (Regrets had never been his style.) The brief call, John told me, brought back "all his hyperbole, his exaggerated self-importance and his embellishment of fact to make himself look grand." Yet their talk reminded him "how badly I had needed that kind of dominating, patriarchal presence when I was younger, and how little I felt 'owned' by my own father in an emotional sense." He remained grateful for all the affection that Scott had given him which with time outweighed the acrimony, the abuse, the stolen photographs, and the black eye.

Scott and John spoke several more times, Scott still unapologetic, still urging John to return because "we owe it to ourselves." He remained estranged from his wife and son, and the rest of his family seldom visited, though he did have at least one dinner with his brother Tom. Scott said his brother admitted: "You were right." He didn't mean about everything of course, but specifically about the recognition of gay people in Canada, the public acknowledgement of our humanity, our mortality.

Scott's Anglican funeral service at St. Thomas's was accompanied by clouds of frankincense and every rite in the book—entirely appropriate, one parishioner remarked, as Scott was convinced he would be with the saints. At the Massey College reception afterwards, old friends and acquaintances reminisced. One woman recalled being in grade seven with Scott and going to a party with him and another child. Scott, she said, played the accordion at the time. He painted the other kids' faces and had them jump about all evening, telling them "I'll be the organ grinder and you can be the monkeys!" I related the old classmate's story to John in San Diego. He replied that "it is as good a metaphor of Scott's life as any. In both his life and his writing he portrayed others by painting a false face on them, and then had them dance to his tune, calling them monkeys, which is how they appeared to him."

What drew me to Scott Symons in the first place? He and I were both idiosyncratic writers going our own way, both speaking and naming the Love that Dare Not, writing about what Scott called "homosentience" in the then-thawing emotional climate of the True North. More than that, both of us fell head over heels in love with spectacularly beautiful, quite unusual seventeen-year-olds who strolled, or strode, into our arms. But Scott was bound to his native Canada in ways that I, as an immigrant, could not be. Scott could never put Rosedale behind him, or the Pink Lady, or his betrayal of boyhood love. Rather, they remained the centre of a psychic world in which he was "eternally thirteen," eternally being told his cock was dirty.

Rating writers is a futile academic exercise. We have no idea how the future will judge our contemporaries. All we know is that we would almost certainly be surprised. Many of the best-known Canadian authors are, though entirely worthy of respect, nonetheless just a tad on the boring side. Scott, on the other hand, was a literary high roller with an utterly unique voice. His name is high on the alternate list with Émile Nelligan, Emily Carr, Grey Owl, Brion Gysin, Juan Butler, bp Nichol, Albert Collignon, bill bissett, Norman Elder, Thomson Highway, Lawrence Ytzhak Braithwaite.... What a roster! Self-starters and visionaries all.

Canadians of course, had seen something like Scott's bombastic mythologizing before, in the robust figure of Irving Layton. But through all Layton's boasts—including his claim to have been born circumcised, the sure sign of a messiah—we could see, or thought we could see, the twinkle in the poet's eye. Scott was every bit as megalomaniacal as Layton, but those black, beady little eyes did not twinkle. Indeed, they seemed (until near the end) not so much searching as accusatory, inquisitorial, confrontational. As for his chequered career (or rather careers, as he had several), Jack McClelland stated it as simply as anyone: "The problem as we see it is that (Scott's) lack of discipline is killing him both as a man and as a writer." His towering ambition attempted the well-nigh impossible: to be the exalted ruler and the insurgent rebel, the hierophant and the heretic, at the same time—a precarious double act attempted by many, Wilde, Mayakovsky, Capote and Mapplethorpe among them. Most came to grief.

Such artists belong to a class of human beings the French call *les monstres sacrés,* sacred monsters. They are compulsively, often prolifically creative creatures, utterly self-absorbed, confident of their own charismatic genius, oblivious to the feelings of others, uncaring or unaware about the effects of their own words or actions. They can be bombastic and demanding. They are often profligate with money, sex, drugs, travel, religion: with them, it is all or nothing. At their most monstrous, they can be paranoid, bullying, "a must to avoid."

Picasso, Hemingway, Frederick Rolfe "Baron Corvo," Aleister Crowley and Ayn Rand are remembered as classic sacred monsters of their century. Scott Symons was surely of their number, which is why Robert Fulford's *mot juste* drew blood. Of his fellow monsters, it may be the dreaded Rolfe whom Scott most resembles—in his not quite definable talent, his enormous sense of entitlement, his unerring capacity for self-sabotage.

The English writer Daniel Farson had the dubious privilege of knowing more than a few such Monsters, including Francis Bacon and Brendan Behan, and in his book *Sacred Monsters* (Bloomsbury, 1988) he succinctly summed them all up: "They may be difficult, temperamental, occasionally treacherous, frequently drunk, usually unpredictable; this is their price for making life more interesting for the rest of us. They are worth the trouble."

Scott Symons certainly made peoples' lives more interesting, for better or worse. He was a unique writer. And at a signal time in the country's history, he presented us with a reminder that there are many Canadas, not all of them yet mapped. He was the féderaste par excellence. He was no saint. But he may well be with them—in one capacity or another.

Sacred Monsters
ALEC BUTLER

T he cover of the book is unforgettable, at least the edition I read in school almost 40 years ago. It is a work of art in itself, the pink border is shocking, in the middle of the cover the mess of erratic blue, black and red lines drawn by someone as if in a fit of rage. I wondered, what was this monstrosity? Picking the book off the top of the stack of identical copies on the teacher's desk I sat down at my desk to take a good look at what I had in my hands. It took a few seconds, then I realized I was looking at a screaming face. I could not imagine what this gruesome cover had to do with what was inside on the pages. Reading it you didn't find out till near the end of *Mad Shadows*, this brilliant book by Marie-Claire Blais, why the face was screaming.

The striking cover art represents one of the most shocking scenes in the book. Expertly built up with tension it is the aftermath of a moment of pure horror, wrought by the talent of the seventeen-year-old author. Right away I discerned that this young writer, my own age at the time she wrote it, had the uncanny ability to make understandable the madness of an unloved child. Isabelle-Marie is as ugly as her brother Patrice is beautiful and as smart as her brother is stupid. The reader is led to the moment when the narcissist, the "beautiful beast" in the title of the original in the author's mother tongue, is horribly disfigured. The face screaming in pure torment makes sense.

The main character of this queer tale is a monster, living in the shadow of a surreally beautiful brother who gets all the attention from their vain mother. The brilliant writing lays out the reason for the impulses that drive the main character, Isabelle-Marie, the beautiful beast's ugly sister, to a point where she shoves Patrice's face into a pan of boiling water. The horror of the moment is heightened by the depth of compassion one feels for this sacred monster.

The mother is also a monster because of her lack of love for her child, begetting the monster that is Isabelle-Marie. But the mother's self-centred, almost normal monster status is stupid, while Isabelle-Marie's monster is rendered as sacred because she is the only character in the book who really suffers. For Blais, suffering is sacred and this was a potent message to hear, because according to the laws of nature I was also a monster because I was queer.

The book was assigned by a twenty-seven-year-old English teacher who was the spitting image of David Cassidy, a pop idol of 1970s on the TV show "The Partridge Family." Back in the day rumour had it that David Cassidy was gay, because he posed in *The Rolling Stone* in a controversial photo that sealed his gay "cred" forever. All the boys in class called the new teacher a "faggot" behind his back, mostly because of the way he dressed. I thought his bell-bottom corduroy brown suit and pink tie were a refreshing break from the red and black plaid and faded blue dungarees worn by everyone else. It didn't seem to matter that the English teacher was married to another teacher, who was a double for Susan Dey, who played David Cassidy's sister on the TV show. That set tongues wagging.

In *The Rolling Stone* photo, a sweetly smiling David Cassidy posed fully clothed, wearing a coat and sweater. In the photo he is leaning back on his elbows on a double bed with a headboard in the background. Was the bed made or unmade? I can't remember. What I do remember, and what no one can ignore, is the outline of a huge hard-on straining against his tight light brown corduroy jeans.

In the 1970s, a well-endowed David Cassidy was sensational news in the press, considering his reputation as the star of a "family" show watched by mostly teenage girls. But not a whisper of this scandal made it to our television screens where the straightness of his character in the family show was undisturbed.

It was amazing that this photo was even snapped by a photographer, much less published. The actual photo, if I remember correctly, is soft core compared to the waves of erect cocks that flood the Internet these days. It is actually a sweet picture of David Cassidy's trademark vacuous smile and is certainly well lit. Dragging one's eyes south to gaze at David's crotch there was a huge curved dick straining the material of his corduroys for all to drool over. Only a "fruit" would flaunt his huge cock like that. This ridiculous reasoning was the logic of the day. I remember my best friend in high school, no doubt a future drag queen, laughing in response to student jibes in the hallways at rural route high, "They're just jealous!"

It was 1976 when I read the stunning story of Isabelle-Marie, a girl who was a monster, because of what she did to her brother. The rural route high school I attended bussed all my peers from deep in the bush. The back woods of the east coast were just as gothic as the setting for *Mad Shadows*. I could imagine this scene happening in the kitchen of the weathered farmhouse of the illegal pig farm just down the road, where rumour had it the brothers and their sister indulged in orgies in the middle of the kitchen floor every Saturday night while the "family" men came from out of the deep bush and stood around in a circle watching the live sex show, tossing 10 dollar bills on the kitchen table afterwards.

When I first read *Mad Shadows* which was originally published in 1959, the year of my birth, I deeply identified with this gothic horror story coming from the mind of someone who was close to my own age when she wrote it quickly in ten days. At seventeen, I was also an aspiring writer, the same age Blais was when she wrote this nightmare of jealousy and rage. It was something beyond sibling rivalry and hate, and the worst case of bad mothering in all of literature. After reading the book I was hooked on Marie-Claire Blais's writing, and I was convinced Blais was also queer, like me. She saw things behind the mask of civility that I could see too, the violence just waiting to erupt in the hallways at a rural route high, mostly towards me, whom they called "sick" and "queer."

We were lucky to have picked up that copy of *Mad Shadows* on that fateful day in English class. I remember most of my classmates were so disturbed by the book that many refused to read it at first. There was a discussion in the class the next day about why the new teacher had assigned the book. Then he impatiently explained that it was to expose us to one of our country's greatest writers, who came from a different background than most writers did, that Blais's working class background was much like our own, that she had to work hard against great odds to be taken seriously after this book was published. That we too could accomplish what Blais did if we wanted to be writers. When the teacher said this I swear he was looking right at me.

The next book I read was *The Manuscripts of Pauline Archange*, a more solid, realistic work, described by critics as Blais's "spiritual autobiography." The book recounts the struggles of Pauline, a working-class girl who wants to become a writer more than anything. In her story I saw again a reflection of my own journey as a working-class queer kid who wanted to be an artist more than anything.

The scene in the book where Pauline's working class father makes fun of her as she sits writing at the kitchen table was one that played out at my own kitchen table at home. To read that passage I saw myself reflected for the first time. I was sure that we had more in common than being working-class writers. The pressure at home to conform, to treat my passion as a hobby, to get serious about how to make a living when I left home was overwhelming, to the point where I took to my room more and more, feeling ashamed, feeling like a freak, feeling useless. To be an artist was worse than being lazy, and to add queerness to the mix was even more damning. Writing was considered an unnatural act. Might as well be both, the two words were interchangeable in my family's eyes, being "queer" didn't necessarily refer to one's sexuality in my world. But more than that it marked one as weird, like a monster is marked by their grandiose emotions and unnatural acts.

Finding proof that confirmed that Blais was queer wasn't easy. Few articles mentioned Blais's private life, except to say she lived with "friends" in a farmhouse outside Montreal. Three years later in 1979, *Nights in the Underground* was published. The book was set in a lesbian bar in Montreal and there was a lot of media coverage in print and on CBC radio. I finally felt vindicated, I felt I had a soulmate out there in the world.

On May 14, 1979, Don Harron interviewed Blais on his radio show Morningside on CBC and I lovingly taped the interview on my double cassette tape player/ radio and later transcribed every word into my beloved black notebook, along with a *Maclean's* article from September 1975 written by Margaret Atwood that I cut out and glued onto the ruled pages. The hardcover black notebook included excerpts from her novels and her one play and poems that I had carefully written out by hand. Beside these excerpts were black and white photos cut from other magazines that were glued beside the excerpts. The photos were dramatic images of children in trouble, drug addicts and prostitutes and other marginalized people, to illustrate Blais's gritty descriptions of life on the margins of society.

Back in the bush where I was growing up, *Books in Canada* magazine arrived with the Saturday paper every week. This slight magazine was a lifeline to the work of other writers and I looked forward to every issue. The February 1979 issue that reviewed *Nights in the Underground* was highly anticipated. The title was "I am, simply, a writer" written by John Hofsess. I devoured the interview with Blais and the excerpts from the book that followed the interview.

To describe the feeling that came over me when my eyes fell on the following quote, highlighted, sticking out like a declaration in the left column of the two-column article, sticking out bigger and bolder than the rest of the typography was pure elation.

"When I asked her why none of the articles about her over the years...have mentioned that the most important relationship of her adult life has been with Mary Meigs, she replied: 'I guess they do not feel comfortable with the truth.'"

I felt vindicated in my faith that this prolific, award-winning writer was queer!

The declaration made my heart beat faster and stronger. It made me grin from ear to ear, but then the whole premise of the article was to support the following assertion by Blais:

"I don't mind being known as gay," she said. "But I don't want to be a 'gay writer.' Anymore than I want to be known as a 'woman writer' or a 'Quebecoise writer.' They are all little boxes. I am simply, a writer, and sometimes I write about Quebec, or about women, or about gay people, but nothing, I feel, fences me in."

I was confused, I was hoping for a more strident declaration of pride in her sexuality and how it informed her work. I had hoped she would stake a claim for a queer aesthetic, showing me the way to forge ahead. I had hoped for what was impossible because I too bristled at being called a "lesbian" writer in the 1990s when my play *Black Friday* was nominated for the Governor General's Award for English drama, back when I was a dyke. And now since I have "transitioned" I bristle at being called a "trans" writer, I guess I also bristle at being fenced in. My need to understand Blais's point of view at the time was great, but was it her duty to stake that claim?

Now here is where things get complicated. Did I crave proof of my own experience of being queer through her work, because my queerness helped me see the colonized mind in action all around me? Did this help me understand the closed mind that condemns difference to the margins? Is this how she felt about her own sexuality, that it opened up her imagination to this awareness of the very "queer" world we had to survive in as sexual minorities?

I realize now that the answers lay in her work, *Nights in the Underground*, a masterpiece about being a gay woman in a straight world. It is a beautiful love story between women who love women, as well as a loving portrait of an older generation of lesbian women, but it does not come close to the gritty heights of her novel *David Sterne*, the story of a thief and rapist, or her fourteen other novels that are so surreal in their level of grit that they are real. A fact critics are often quick to point out is that she is one of a handful of prolific women writers whose protagonists are mostly male. This is another interesting fact about Blais's work that fascinates me as a writer, her bravery in crossing those gender boundaries was admirable.

At the time I was stuck in the middle between the two acceptable genders it was possible to be in the 1970s. I felt like a teenage boy but I was called a "lesbian" and a "dyke" in the hallways at school. I knew what a "lesbian" was, but was that what I was? I read about Sappho and her school of devotees on the Isle of Lesbos in the encyclopedia, but is that where I belonged? I was constantly falling in love with girls, especially the tough girls who hung out around the back door before first period smoking joints, getting us high, sometimes even making out with us, but ignoring us in the locker-lined hallways. I wanted to experience the love Blais wrote about in *Nights in the Underground*, but it was questionable whether I was even a woman, did I deserve such love? When I heard Don Harron interview my favourite writer, I was reassured when he pointed out at the beginning of the interview that the love Blais writes about in this novel about women loving women is "universal."

My ears really pricked up when Harron brought up what he calls the "transvestite theme" adding that sometimes the masculine and the feminine in a person is what interests people and Blais agreed enthusiastically that "this double nature is very important." It was not the first time hearing that word "transvestite"; it was a word that scared me and shamed me. I wanted to wear boys' clothes from a young age and fought wearing dresses, I knew I was what this word described and this was the first experience of hearing this word in a positive context. It was a revelation. The "double nature" that Blais spoke of that morning on the radio was like a light going on in my head, this was my nature, to be both male and female. This person who I admired but had never met saw me for the first time; it was a gift of insight that gave me confidence that I was on the right path, as rough as it was.

The *Books in Canada* interview even provided a much-needed physical description of Blais, "Her dust jacket and other public photographs do not do her justice, possibly because she refuses to be vain about her appearance. In real life she is hauntingly beautiful; it is not the skin-deep sort of beauty that disintegrates with age, but rather some radiance that speaks of and to the mind. There are moments when her eyes seem to be filled with all the sadness in the world (200-odd years of Quebec history, 2000 years of women's history, and the whole sorry business of mankind), but then, remembering some outlandish anecdote or taking another sip of wine, she will suddenly beam with energy, her androgynous face triumphant with impassioned life"(Hofsess, 1979).

The description of Blais as androgynous and not concerned with her appearance was compelling, satisfying proof that she was different from other women, not concerned with make-up or fashion, in an era where beehive hairdos were still the norm. This was code that Blais was queer like me. I avoided all things feminine like the plague from a young age, rebelling against the female designation that was checked off on my birth certificate, physically fighting not to be put in dresses since I was a toddler.

Reading this article I realized I too had never been concerned with attracting male attention like other female designated people who were in my class at school. The girls in high school willingly conformed to gender expectations while I was called "sick" and "queer" in those nasty rural route high school hallways. I was born different, medical texts of the day stated that the gender I expressed in how I dressed was in opposition to my female designation. This was "against nature," according to the doctors my parents took me to when I started having a menstrual cycle and growing a beard at age 12. According to the "science" of the day I was abnormal, technically I was a "monster" too. Could this be why I identified so strongly with so many of Blais's stories? Her sense of humour was akin to the sharp, biting humour one develops while facing the gallows; being queer also sharpens one's sense of humour; having nothing to lose equals freedom to be one's self.

Reading about Blais in *Books in Canada* I had proof that I was not the only one transgressing gender. Back then it was easier for men like my English teacher to get away with having long hair than it was for young women to have beards. A description provided by Atwood in the September 1975 *Maclean's* article of Blais wearing the same denim "pant suit," the three times they met for the interview was a red flag. Before pant suits became an anti-fashion statement, Joan of Arc was my only example of a female designated person wearing male clothing. Women wearing pant suits were a signal that one was a radical in the 1970s.

Reading Atwood's article about meeting Blais and her assumptions about the writer was educational. The theme of the article was how a writer reflects on their reputation in the real world. Blais's response to a question from another interviewer asking if she had ever been "male homosexual" like the protagonist of her novel *The Wolf,* was simply, "not yet." I read this interview around the same time I read Blais's first two books. It was eye opening even if there were few hints about Blais's private life. The article was rich, drawing a portrait of this fascinating writer. Atwood never explicitly outs Blais; one has to read between the lines, as they say, code for a "gay" subtext in those early post-Stonewall days. Even so on this slender evidence Blais in her dark blue denim pant suit became my modern day hero. My image of her as an Amazon-like figure came into focus, my attraction to her complex, layered writing, grew more intense. *The Manuscripts of Pauline Archange* is the most relentlessly realistic of her novels, to the point of naturalism. Four years later hearing Blais talk about her theory of how important a "double nature" was for an artist on national radio was an inspiration on how to be different, how to be queer. There was a light at the end of the tunnel at last.

"Despite what some critics regard as the morbidity of her characters and subject material, it seems to have gone unnoticed that her attitude to even the most grotesque cruelties in human nature is never one of pessimism. The Blais sensibility is composed principally of keen clinical interest; and for the rest, for all that passes beyond understanding, a generous pardon"(Hofsess, 1979).

In her novels, her play, and her poetry Blais describes human suffering and depravity in great detail. She was especially great at describing the suffering of abandoned children. I felt she was describing my life growing up in the bush, the back roads of my neighbourhood were filled with haunted abandoned graveyards where Victorian-era farmhouses were unapproachable, because howling packs of dogs drove one away, even if one were looking for help. While Blais described so much of my reality, she was never a pessimist. The reason I read and reread Blais's books was to figure out how to get through my own situation of hopelessness, loneliness, and despair. I was growing up trying to love life despite all the bullying. Constantly being asked every day if I was a boy or girl, not because anyone cared to know but because my tormentors believed "I was neither one nor the other," "you don't belong here, go away," was exhausting. But there was nowhere to go, except into the imagination, my own and Blais's. Not surprisingly my own early attempts at writing were pretty much similar to her style: it was a way of finding my voice. I was becoming a writer.

Hofsess wrote, "She could have been a different sort of writer—one who lies, in her fiction as well as interviews. She could have remained a prestigious writer, her life one thing, her art another. But instead she is seeking to integrate her life and work, to become whole and in touch with her deepest needs and feelings. 'How fiercely we aspired to live freely, in harmony of happy minds and bodies,' she wrote in *The Manuscripts of Pauline Archange*. Each generation has the same dreams when it is young; and each generation becomes washed up and useless when those who comprise it lose the fire of such dreams. Blais aligns herself with the youth because she still believes in the intense desirability of social change."

From a young age I saw a need for society to change. I wanted to be a story teller and a truth teller. While some believe one can be one or the other, but not both, as if story telling is inherently based on a lie because stories are "made up," I knew when I read this paragraph this was the way to proceed, to integrate my life and work, to be in touch with my deepest needs and feelings, which never lie.

Sources

Stafford, Philip. *Marie-Claire Blais: Canadian Writers & their works* (Forum House: 1971).

Atwood, Margaret. "Marie-Claire Blais is not for burning" in *Maclean's Magazine* (September, 1975).

Hofsess, John. "I am, simply, a writer," in *Books in Canada*, (February, 1979).

Transcripts of Marie-Claire Blais, the CBC Morningside Interview with Don Harron (May 14, 1979).

LOOK
ANNE FLEMING

Our dorm room door had a picture of Kirk and Spock on it and was almost always unlocked. It was what you did at Renison College, you left your door unlocked, or better yet, open. That was how things worked. If you were home, your door was open. Evenings were open doors and the hum of work done or avoided, typewriters typing, highlighters highlighting, popcorn popped in hot-air poppers and spritzed with water from spray bottles so the salt had something to stick to. People grew listless and wandered down the hall to chat, to complain about their courses, their essays, their friends or their families, their boyfriends or lack of boyfriends, to talk about the news, to ask about assignments or listen to reggae or borrow a pen or a typewriter or paper.

It was my second year. The year before, I'd assumed, against all evidence to the contrary, that I was straight. When I got a letter from a friend saying, "I have come to terms with my sexuality; I am a lesbian," I wrote back that my one heterosexual encounter had been satisfactory.

If you're wondering who was Spock in the picture on the door, and who was Kirk, well, let me just say, "Live long and prosper." Was Chris like Kirk? Chris had charm, verve, impetuousness and warmth. Yeah, I guess she was like Kirk.

I had spent every day of May and June not realizing I was in love. I just had a really, really good friend I spent every minute with, whose soccer games I went to, whose parents' basement I stayed up late watching surreal Japanese movies in, who skipped high school to sit on my parents' back porch, who took me to Yorkville cafés.

She gave me a book to read. Radclyffe Hall's *The Well of Loneliness*. I read it that night, the whole thing, murmuring her name. Finished at three in the morning, I gave it back the next day. "Good book. Thanks."

In case you've never read *The Well of Loneliness* and the title doesn't give it away, it's a taut and depressing tale of a woman, Stephen, raised by her father as a boy, who discovers she is an invert. She falls in love, and gives up her lover to the man she truly deserves. I don't know who I thought was Stephen, me or Chris. We were both boyish, bookish, athletic.

I should have known then I was in love. I should have been able to say to myself if to no one else, "I am in love. This is what this tightness in the chest is, this thrill at the prospect of seeing another's face, hearing her voice." "Good book," I said. "Thanks."

A month later I headed up north to my summer job and (not-quite realized) through a hollowness in my chest about the same size and shape as the former tightness how keenly I missed her, how there must be, oh, never mind. And then she joined me. There was a back rub. A kiss. A sudden knowledge: I was a lesbian.

I did not know any lesbians except the friend who had come out via letter the year before. It is hard to overstate how completely unthinkable being a lesbian was for me in 1983, and I was such an obvious lesbian. You would have thought if anyone figured it out it would have been me. When I did figure it out, though, there was no hesitation, no waffling. A giant lock went *thunk* and hinged open. My whole life made sense.

Chris was ahead of me. She had already had a lover, had already taken Jane Rule's *Lesbian Images* out of the library, had already embarked on a reading program (along with Radclyffe Hall were Violet Trefusis, Vita Sackville-West, and Violette LeDuc—clearly having a V name was a prerequisite for lesbian authorship). But our need for secrecy was high. We were young: nineteen and eighteen. We worked at a children's camp. Our families were conservative, mine especially, and already profoundly suspicious of my masculinity. People lost their jobs, we knew, for being lesbians. They lost their housing. Their families disowned them. Sent them to psych wards.

In the fall I worked at an all-night grocery in Toronto. Chris worked in the mailroom at a law office downtown. I got in touch with the friend who had come to terms with her sexuality. She was kick-starting a career as a lesbian folk singer. Her lover—that was the word we were suddenly using, that was the word it took less time than you'd think to get used to, that was what we were—worked at the Toronto Women's Bookstore, where you could buy lesbian books and womyn's music and jewellery in the shape of labryses—double-headed axes as wielded, word had it, by Amazons. We went to lesbian dances at the Ukrainian Cultural Centre. We went to lesbian potlucks at the Centre for Christian Studies, with women fifteen and twenty years older than us. We went to the Cameo Club. We went to the lesbian section of the library.

Come winter, we moved into residence together in Waterloo. Finally, we could really be together instead of tensely poised in our parents' houses, listening for someone's return, or tucked into a dark corner of a park. Only now we were tensely poised in our residence room, listening for someone at the open door. We did a lot of flinging ourselves apart at slight noises. Each night, we pushed our single beds together. Each morning, we pulled them apart.

Each Thursday at six, we turned on the radio. We heard a creaking door, mock-spooky laughter, mock-spooky piano music and the chorus: *Here come the lezz-bi-a-ans, here come the leaping lesbians.* It was *The Leaping Lesbian Show* on CKMS-FM, listener-supported radio. *Ah-ah-ah, don't look in the closet, ah-ah-ah, who's creeping down the stairs?* When our hall mates knocked and entered, we lunged for the radio dial trying to look like we were not lunging for the radio dial. We willed our visitors to leave so we could turn *The Leaping Lesbians* back on. So we could listen to love songs sung by women to women. To Cris Williamson filling up and spilling over, Margie Adam tap dancing on the moon, Meg Christian calling up and hanging up on her high school gym teacher. So we could listen to the community event listings, which weren't many. There was a LOOK meeting once a month. LOOK, the Lesbian Organization of Kitchener. The acronym struck us as funny, but, "We should go," we said. "Definitely."

We didn't go.

We went to classes, we ate in the cafeteria, we made jokes with our floor mates, we ate popcorn. We closed our door and kissed. We closed the door. We pushed the beds together. We pulled the beds apart. We tuned in on Thursdays.

Although we had been to those lesbian dances and bars and were making our way through the lesbian canon, although we were captivated by lesbian subculture, I was still nervous to go to lesbian events. It was daring simply to go to an event where you didn't know anybody. It was an act of double-daring to go to a lesbian event where you didn't know anybody. We kept saying we were going and then not going.

Then one cold, cold winter's night in February, we went. I had got a winter coat from the thrift shop, my first men's coat. It had a herringbone pattern, big ugly lapels, a double-breasted hip-length cut and pockets, I discovered too late, that smelled faintly of barf. I washed them out as best I could, hung the coat outside to air, and tried to remember not to put my hands in the pockets. On my feet I wore cheap suede Peter Pan boots.

It was about minus twenty-five. The meeting was at somebody's house. We had the address and a map. We took the bus and got off at the wrong stop, went down this street and that street, getting colder and colder. My feet froze. My nose, susceptible to frostbite since I was a kid, turned white. We turned corners, backtracked, turned the other way, and finally found the square limestone three-storey house.

"Is this it? Do you think this is it?"

"I think this is it."

"All right. Let's go meet us some lesbo-killer-dykes." We called all lesbians lesbo-killer-dykes, including ourselves.

"You sure?"

"Sure I'm sure. Are you sure?"

"No, I'm sure. I just want to make sure you're sure."

"I'm sure."

"Okay."

"Okay."

"Let's go."

"Let's go."

Still we stood there for a moment, our breath hanging in the air.

The apartment was on the third floor of the house. We creaked up the stairs (ah-ah-ah, who's creeping down the stairs?), knocked on the door, not knowing quite what we were going to find on the other side. What we found were Marlene Dietrich posters, cats, cigarette smoke, a broken furnace, a feeble heater, lesbians in winter jackets, politics, laughter. What we found was welcome.

We already knew some of their voices from the radio, Moe's crisp and quick and didactic, Lyne's warm and mellow and thoughtful. And here they were in the flesh. Under layers of coats. Moe wore a lot of silver rings and sat with a presiding tone in a vintage armchair. Paula, in a puffy down jacket and laughing eyes, perched on an arm of the chair, her hand on Moe's shoulder. Lyne was on the couch. Even before she hugged you, Lyne was like a hug waiting to happen. I wasn't a hugger. I didn't know how to hug. Hugging? What the hell?

There were other women there—one with square shoulders and square glasses and wry comments, another in a floppy patchwork suede cap over hippy hair. We were younger than they were by about ten years. They half ignored us, half drew us in. They talked and smoked and laughed and drank tea. They had a vision of a better future.

I called Lyne up recently to see what she could tell me about LOOK. Who started it? When? What did it do, other than hold meetings like the one we had gone to? She didn't know who had started it. Maybe this woman who'd worked at the leftist press? All she knew was it was already in swing when she'd arrived in town. But first, she'd been involved with LOON—Lesbians of Ottawa Now—and LOOT—the Lesbian Organization of Toronto.

I'd already known about LOOT from Becki Ross's book, *The House that Jill Built*, an oral history of the years LOOT was in operation. Knowing of LOOK and LOOT, I imagined if I dug a little I would find there were groups like this all over the country: there'd be LOOP in Peterborough, LOOS in Saskatoon, LOOD in Dartmouth—everywhere, lesbians who organized. I wasn't exactly right and I wasn't exactly wrong. There was no LOOP that I could find, no LOOS, but there was LOGO (Guelph, Ontario), there was ELF (Edmonton Lesbian Feminists), there was Vancouver Lesbian Connection, the "house on Smith Street" in Saskatoon, there was Labyris Montréal. Lyne had basically done a little east-west tour of Southern Ontario lesbian organizations, LOON, LOOT, LOOK

LOOT operated out of a brick house at 142 Jarvis Street. "Going into the building," Lyne told me, "I saw a poster: 'Are You a Thespian?'—and I thought, 'Oh my god, lesbians in theatre!'" Through LOOT, Lyne met Keltie Creed, who would later start Womynly Way Productions to bring lesbian acts to Toronto. Through LOOT, she got a part in a play by Québecoise writer Jovette Marchessault. Lyne went on to stage manage at a number of different women's music festivals. She fell in love with the fact that women did everything: built the stage, hung the lights, ran the sound board, wrote, produced, performed. She fell in love with lesbian feminism, with lesbian culture.

After Toronto, Lyne made her way a little farther west to Kitchener-Waterloo, where LOOK was already in swing. Through LOOK, she met the women who became her roommates on the farm outside of town. Through her roommates on the farm, she met the woman who lived up the road. Lynn. Lyne and Lynn. They've been together thirty-four years now. They got married a couple of years ago. They're looking forward to retirement.

The week after the LOOK meeting, Lyne and Lynn picked us up at Renison to take us out to the farm. Lynn had short hair and a lopsided grin, work pants and Sorel boots.

The pair of them looked out of place at Renison—dykey and unapologetic. I liked that.

As we got farther out of town, the snow banks grew higher, the snow whiter, the world quieter. After about twenty minutes, we pulled into a classic Southern Ontario farmhouse, the same limestone-based yellow brick as all the local buildings.

Inside was a big L-shaped living-room-dining-room-kitchen with old couches and a farm table, but we mostly hung out in a smaller den off the living room where a space heater could keep us warm. The place was draughty, run down and excellent. I fell immediately in love with it.

It wasn't exactly a lesbian commune. It wasn't "lesbian land," something we'd never heard of before but were starting to now. But it was a community. Paula lived there, too (though these days she was often at Moe's), and the woman with the suede cap, Becky, and Becky's twelve-year-old daughter, and two dogs and three cats, including the kitten, Norma Jean, or Noodge, who launched herself claws out because she never landed where she aimed.

We ate dinner, we told stories. Ours were about conservative, middle-class North Toronto, about camp, about the teen who'd said to Chris, "Well, you and Fleming are dykes, right?" which was the first time I'd even heard the word. (Chris: "No, no, no." But how sad that she couldn't have said yes.) Theirs were about women's music festivals, Michigan and NEWMR, which artist was like what backstage (Odetta: a diva, Ferron: particular) or about Lynn's farming family or any of the hundreds of things people talk about when they first get to know each other. We stayed overnight in a double bed piled high with quilts. A double bed. No pushing anything together, no pulling apart. When we left the next day, the Lynns hugged us goodbye.

"Fleming, you're like a tree," said Lyne.

"I'm not much of a hugger."

"Oh, you will be. We're going to train you." She leaned forward on her toes, tapped me on the back, barely touching. "This is a straight-girl hug."

"The A-frame," said Lynn.

"And this," Lyne said, wrapping her arms around me and bringing her full torso against mine, "is a lesbian hug." She squeezed.

Gradually, I learned to hug. Gradually, I started to say "woman" instead of "girl" or "chick" (ironic) or "lady." Behind the dorm room door, I learned to be less Spock-like. I began to recognize I had feelings and even identify which ones they were. Oh, look, it's insecurity. Oh, that one, that one's resentment. Hey, tenderness. Joy. Anger. Compassion. Chris and I came out to our friends at Renison. We stopped having to lunge for the radio dial.

In the summer term, I worked in Algonquin Park as a canoe guide. Chris worked in Toronto. She met a woman who worked at a group home in our parents' neighbourhood and had a mini-fling with her.

At summer's end, in the city, the day we were due to head back to Waterloo to share an apartment off campus with another friend, my father came into my room in the morning, saw the previous day's haircut, and said, "Now is the time of life you could get into the seedy lesbian lifestyle, Anne."

Great. Thanks, Dad. I'll keep that in mind.

He went to work and Mom came in to ask if I was gay with Chris and I said yes and what followed was crappy and a much longer story but it helped to know that Lyne and Lynn were there, LOOK was there, lesbians existed, by tens and by thousands, and they were making space for themselves, and I could be part of that, I was part of that. The personal was political. The political was personal.

Chris had three or four more flings before we broke up a few years later (which doesn't tell the story of our relationship at all). We're still friends. Lyne and Lynn consoled me through the break-up. I'd meet Lynn at the greenhouse on campus where she worked and we'd go fishing out in the country on her lunch break. LOOK hosted dances and coffeehouses. I read poetry at one of them. I started hosting *The Leaping Lesbian* show. Around 1986 or '87, Moe moved back to Nelson, and LOOK folded. The radio show kept going until 1999.

The call for submissions to this anthology said the book would be a collection of essays about "famous queer Canadians who were pioneers in forging an LGBTQ identity and creating an LGBTQ community in Canada." I had a lot of ideas who I could honour—Jovette Marchessault, Heather Bishop, Mary Meigs—and then I thought about LOOK and all the organizations like it. I thought I'd be able to find out more about LOOK, thought I'd be able to weave its history into my own story, but in a way it's kind of perfect that I don't know who started it. They're not famous. Famous people gave us rallying points and voices to latch onto, words to read, songs to sing. But it's the unfamous I want to celebrate here. They weren't perfect, these organizations. Still, they carved out space. Lyne likes to tell the story of the two women from Mount Forest, a smaller community up near Orangeville, who made sure to come into town for groceries on Thursdays. They'd sit in the Zehr's parking lot at Waterloo Town Square, turn on the radio, hear that creaking door, the spooky laughter. *Here come the lesbians. Here come the leaping lesbians.* They'd fill up, and head home.

I Got Schooled
GORDON BOWNESS

"Are you sure you've never done this before?" After years and years of dread and thwarted desire, of hoping for this very moment, finally, I was giving a man a blowjob. And I had just gotten the best compliment ever.

Let's just say I was ready. I was 27, a late bloomer.

That man, my first lover—my first male lover—was Garth Barriere, a handsome eccentric who worked selling junk and antiques. We were roughly the same age. This was 1991 in Toronto. I had known Garth for a few months before working up enough nerve, and drinking enough booze, to follow him home late one night after a party.

He broke up with me one week later. A libertine who knew what he wanted from sex, Garth had no patience for an entanglement with such a romantic and sexual novice like I then was. In almost the same breath as ending our affair, he announced that we would be great pals and that I must meet this fascinating group of gay men he'd just befriended, drag queens who had a troupe called The Boho Girls. They had parties every weekend. I simply must go.

That's how I got to 341 Seaton Street, an '80s townhouse in Lower Cabbagetown, the poorer, scrappier extension to fashionable Cabbagetown proper, located a few blocks east of Toronto's gay ghetto along Church Street.

My mentor wasn't a person; it was a scene.

My memory is that I went to the house on my own, that first time. How brazen. How desperate. Again, I must have been ready.

I walked into something right out of a Golden Era Hollywood film, when homosexuals were depicted in all their sleazy pre-equality glory. It was like I was Don Murray in Otto Preminger's *Advise and Consent* walking into Club 602. Heads turning, getting the intense once-over from guys in tight sweaters. But the music playing wasn't Frank Sinatra, more like Pet Shops Boys or Madonna. And I didn't run away in disgust. I came back nearly every weekend for the next six years or so.

It was just a regular Friday night that first time. No drag; that would come later. A small group of friends sat around a large kitchen table at the centre of which was an ashtray the size of a car tire.

The townhouse, a tall spiral built around a central stair-case like a castle tower, was home to David Christopher Richards and Stephen Clark, ex-boyfriends who still lived together. That conjoined twinning of love and antagonism characterized the whole scene that congregated around them.

There was a core group of about eight white men, all in their late 20s or early 30s. They were an odd mix of welfare queens and professionals, artists and waiters and sales staff. They were bright young men with their futures still ahead of them.

David said then—and now—that he consciously wanted to create a type of salon in his home, a coming together of artists and bohemians. Like the gay bars of old, it didn't really matter what you did for a living. What mattered was your conversation, your wit. The place was always loud with talk and laughter and music, the air heavy with smoke and girly testosterone.

The hometowns of the group ranged from Sarnia and North Bay to the Ottawa Valley. Three grew up in Toronto's Scarborough neighbourhood. One was from Montreal's NDG. They had come out as gay and escaped small towns and suburbs years before I did. They had lived so much already. I was agog.

One fellow had hitchhiked across the country as a teenager, one ridiculous sex-capade after another. He had lived in New York City and performed in drag in the East Village in its grimy heyday. He dropped famous names like spare change: Boy George, Faye Dunaway and Prince Edward. Another fellow would soon have a not-too-secret affair with a not-too-closeted federal cabinet minister. One young man was a certifiable genius with countless degrees and questionable hygiene. He'd tell horoscopes using dodecagonal dice, peering into the future with a glass of red wine rolling against his forehead. Another guy had just been charged with first-degree murder.

You'd think I'd lead an essay like this with the killer drag queen. But he was the most normal of the lot. George Allen, also known as Mama Dominatrix, the Rubenesque star of *The Boho Girls*, worked as a nurse at the Wellesley Hospital. In the fall of 1991, he was part of the care team for a terminally ill man taken off life support at the request of his family. But the man started experiencing distress so George gave him an extra dose of potassium chloride to help speed up the inevitable. When confronted by a superior afterward, George readily admitted what he had done. It's something that happens frequently in hospitals. It was also something George saw as necessary, part of his calling as a nurse: To care for people, to allow them to die with dignity. But his public airing of an open secret awoke a lumbering system of compulsory reporting that went all the way to the police.

George was charged with murder. The hospital, the police, the family of the deceased, no one wanted a trial. But no one could stop it. In a deal worked out a year later, George pleaded guilty to the lesser charge of administering a noxious substance. He didn't do jail time but he did lose his nurse's license. He had to double-down on the drag to make a living, never really part of his life's plan.

So there was one guy in the group charged with murder. Another guy was dying of AIDS. That was Stephen. He died in the summer of 1993. Completing an odd circle, Garth moved into 341 Seaton Street soon after. Stephen had such a fierce hold on life. I remember one evening he had gone out on his own in drag; the makeup and the floppy summer hat helped hide the karposi sarcomas on his face. It was a movie night. The rest of us were watching *The Lion in Winter*, a biting historical epic starring Katharine Hepburn as Eleanor of Aquitaine. Unbeknownst to us, Stephen had returned from the bar, entering the living room at the exact moment Hepburn uttered one of movie's many quotable quotes: "Mother's tired. Come stick pins tomorrow morning. I'll be more responsive then." Stephen delivered the lines in perfect unison. Hilarity.

His passing was not easy; the pain and disfigurement. Thankfully, George was one of his primary caregivers; his grace and skills were sorely needed.

So death stalked us. So what? There was a bottomless 48-ounce bottle of vodka in the freezer and laughs to be had. No, it wasn't all fun and games. Those two tragedies loomed large and dark. And there were others, familial injuries and a variety of wounds. But misfortune and trauma never overwhelmed. Life went on. Life sparkled.

Soon after hooking up with Garth and my introduction to 341 Seaton Street, I was walking downtown. Writer David Bateman happened to cycle by on his bike. He called to me from across the street: "I heard you came out!"

"Yes, I did," I called back happily.

"Go back in," he yelled. "It's horrible out here."

It's hard to explain the mixture of cultural attainment and steely-eyed realism, the flights of fancy and echoes of pain that coursed through gay culture in the 1980s and '90s. AIDS was still killing gay men in droves and cultural commentators and politicians still talked openly about their disgust towards homosexuals. Yet we gays were having the times of our lives.

We gays, how easy it was for me to find my footing. The gang at 341 Seaton accepted me immediately. I was new; there's nothing like fresh meat. I was exotic; I looked nothing like anyone there. I was a follower; I wasn't pushy, that came later. I had a great laugh; I gave good audience.

And I was up for anything.

There was a groove cut into the pavement that ran from 341 Seaton Street along Carlton to Church Street. After an evening of boozing at the house, we'd head out to the bars. Often it was to Woody's for last call and pre-cruising. It was Toronto's big meet-and-greet bar, where *The Boho Girls* often performed; reportedly it had the largest beer sales of any bar, straight or gay, in Canada. Then we'd usually head two blocks south to The Barn for dancing and cruising proper. The three-floor dance club had a great backroom back then, and french-fries! And there'd be more boozing (The Barn served alcohol after hours until the mid-'90s when last call shifted to 2:00 a.m., a move that killed most of the booze-cans downtown). Sometimes we'd head back through Allan Gardens, a lovely park surrounding a Victorian greenhouse, for last-chance cruising in the bushes. Plus maybe a night-cap or two back at the house.

Then there was the drag.

The Boho Girls were a Church Street phenomenon during the early '90s. Unusual for the time, their drag productions weren't just a series of lip-synched pop hits, but shows with whole concepts and stories. Songs, dialogue, narration and sound effects would be pre-recorded onto a mixed tape (this was pre-digital). A technician would press the play button and the troupe lip-synched and performed a whole show in one go. It wasn't unusual for things to go awry... much to the delight of the audience. There were oodles of costume changes off-stage and on. Crazy, inventive stuff. Each of the girls was an inveterate ham. Their shows were outrageous fun.

For Halloween one year, they produced *The All Ghoul Revue*, which had a chorus line of brides of Frankenstein stomping about to "Hey, Big Spender." One Easter saw *The Greatest Boho Story Ever Told*, the climax of which featured the coming of the "Divine One," aka Mama dressed as Divine entering on a shopping cart full of potato chips.

Such antics garnered *The Boho Girls* a cult following, which included me. Sadly, I never got to perform with them. But I did drag with them, often, at Halloween or Pride or just because.

What a revelation.

I was a mess of a drag queen at first. But it didn't matter. The silly mayhem was just so infectious, especially with an experienced and hilarious posse backing me up.

Drag is like a form of therapy. It starts with the shoes. Putting on high-heeled shoes forces you to stand and walk differently; it realigns your posture, it compels you to be physically different in the world. The rest, the makeup, the dresses, is just window dressing. In heels, all your insecurities and self-consciousness fall away. You become powerful, sexy and aggressive. You strut. It's a magical transformation. Theatre folk know what I mean. The power of masks, of playing a part, of accessing alter egos. High heels offer a five-minute crash course in method acting. Your inner diva awakes.

Of course, the makeup, the costumes, the wigs have power too. That stuff is key to how your alter ego is perceived.

Even today, with our pomo-metro-sexual-queer-inclusive culture, there's nothing like a little drag to drive people crazy. Young boys, old ladies, nervous girls—they have to touch the queens. *Monstres sacrés* have an enduring power. It's partly the gender inversion; it's partly the brazen attitude. Audiences, whether in a bar or on the streets, eat it up.

The drag parties on Seaton were a production in themselves: Six to ten guys lined up at long mirrors with lights all around, makeup strewn everywhere, a glue gun simmering away. A number of spectators would join the fun, giddy on the toxic miasma of hairspray, sweaty pantyhose and cigarette smoke. David was often the creative force behind the wardrobe and the look. He could whip up a half dozen costumes in no time flat (and sometimes they'd fall apart just as quickly.) We had some very odd and eccentric themes over the years: the Endoras, the Femmes Noirs, fairies, cocktails, unicorns, boy-crazed cougars, the colour red, ghosts...and they keep coming. There's still a small group of us who love to get together and play dress-up. We actually look forward to the day when we will do drag in mobility scooters. I'm seeing a lot of hooped ball gowns. Imagine the gliding action.

Years later I now make a convincing drag queen, and by convincing I don't mean I look like a girl, I mean I look like a man who knows what he's doing in a dress. It just shows how far I've come. What strange portals have opened up for me since I came out.

Those first gay years offered a heady mix of sex, socializing, politics and culture—mind-altering stuff, especially for a former football star like me, almost fresh from the prairies.

I grew up in Winnipeg. My siblings were all jocks: my two older brothers, my older sister. I didn't have a choice. I became a jock, captain of four championship football teams. Outside of TV and records, there wasn't much culture or art in our house. My erudite and culturally refined father, a scientist and professor, kept his distance; he was English, after all. My vivacious mother, who never finished high school, was sort of an art project herself; an Indian Singaporean marooned in Manitoba. I lived at home with my parents until I was 23, when I moved to Toronto to do a master's in history at the University of Toronto.

Slowly, blindly, I groped my way towards literature and theatre. But it was all a shadow play, empty. I was still in the closet. I hadn't kissed a man. What did I know of love and lust and heartache (other than the unrequited kind)? What did I know of the bloody beating heart of the arts?

I wasn't just hungry for sex; I was hungry for meaning.

One of the more outrageous characters at 341 Seaton Street was John Wimbs, a founding member of *The Boho Girls*. Back in the '90s, John did PR for Garth Drabinsky and got us tickets to all the amazing Livent shows: *Kiss of the Spiderwoman, Show Boat, Fosse, Ragtime.* It was a great education in musical theatre. Finally, the arts moved to the fore in my life. Along with John Kander, Fred Ebb and Chita Rivera, the guys at 341 Seaton Street debated the merits of jazz divas Dinah Washington, Sarah Vaughan and Ella Fitzgerald, or playwrights Sky Gilbert, Tomson Highway and Daniel MacIvor, or writers Paul Monette, Christopher Isherwood and Timothy Findley, or drag queens Rusty Ryan, Michelle Ross and Georgie Girl.

I'm not being perverse in juxtaposing a 300-pound queen like Rusty Ryan with a Governor General's Award-winning writer like Timothy Findley. I don't make great distinctions between high and low art. I learned to appreciate the honesty and hard work of bar entertainers. They can't hide behind heuristic verbiage or social respectability. And I watched as David and John took their hard-won bar stripes into the world of "legitimate" theatre, writing in 1994 a camp-tastic play called *Molly Wood,* inspired by the historical figure Alexander Wood, now considered the gay-founding father of Toronto. John and David won Dora Awards for their efforts.

I got schooled.

Great secrets were unveiled to me at 341 Seaton, revelations in the realm of art ("Everyone has got it wrong. Paul Verhoeven's *Showgirls* is a masterpiece"), swearing ("Jesusfuckingchristupmyass!") and men ("Bad skin? Bad shoes? Great sex").

But the most important secret I learned was how to walk away from all the macho garbage heaped upon me as a closeted brown football player from redneck Winnipeg.

What is liberation? Can you be liberated even when society hates you? The old bromide, "The personal is political," resonates profoundly for those of us who came of age before lesbians and gay men attained our current level of legal equality and social acceptance. Personal liberation was possible before societal liberation. That's what 341 Seaton Street taught me. Party houses, shared homes or apartments passed from friend to friend... such places were critically important, not just on an individual level, but on the level of LGBTQ community-making and history, as important as any bar (and worthy of much more historical research and reporting).

Night after boozy night, we traded stories about ourselves. Whether sexual, romantic or physical, our defeats were celebrated as richly and entertainingly as our successes, in fact, more so. Nothing got the room laughing harder than someone detailing one of their spectacular social fails. Glorious expiation.

Like the time someone decided to experiment with light bondage on a new trick. He had tied their ball sacks together, then promptly fell off his loft bed, pulling his poor yelping companion down with him.

Or the time another guy, who used a little too much eyebrow pencil to disguise his thinning hair, blew a man in the front hallway of his apartment. After a job well done, he stood up and sent the trick on his way. Only then did my friend see the big brown stain on the wall from where the back of his head kept hitting.

Or, in fairness, here's one of mine. After Stephen's funeral, I ended up in a drunken threesome in Vaseline Towers (the popular name for an apartment building in Toronto's ghetto). It was a rather limp affair and two of us got thrown out. But we kept at it in the elevator. We awoke when the elevator started moving again. Somehow passing out half naked in an elevator seemed a fitting tribute to Stephen.

No shame. I felt no shame. For someone who didn't come out until 27, to be able to say that was remarkable. I had become the high-stepping, fun-loving gay I was meant to be. Liberation.

But time marches on. Middle age, boyfriends, substances, careers—the salon petered out as individual group members went their separate ways. The lessons I learned there, however, endure.

Within a year of coming out, I had a regular front-page column in the country's leading gay and lesbian newspaper, *Xtra*. My life had taken another surprising turn: I had become a writer.

In May of 1992, I attended two rallies within 48 hours of each other. The first protested the police raid on the LGBTQ bookstore Glad Day. Owner John Scythes had been charged with obscenity for selling the lesbian SM magazine *Bad Attitude*. It was just one in a long string of attacks on queer bookstores and freedoms of expression.

The second protested the lack of indictments against white LA police officers in the beating of a black man, Rodney King. This was following a four-year period in Toronto that saw police shoot eight black men, four fatally. The year 1992 marked the nadir of relations between police and Toronto's black community. That rally turned violent. Storefronts up and down Yonge Street were smashed. A horse-mounted riot squad was called in.

Those 48 hours left me reeling.

My friend Garth, a former columnist with *Xtra*, suggested I write about my experience and send it in to the paper. More fortuitous advice. I committed to nothing but squirrelled the idea away. I began to write, mostly as a way to understand my feelings. I submitted the story to *Xtra* unsolicited and it got published. So did a second piece, a poetic rumination on the privileged position shared by queers and people of colour. I was called into the *Xtra* offices and offered a regular column. I had become a writer.

Over the next four years, I worked out my thoughts and emotions in print and in public. (I retired the column when I became the arts and entertainment editor of *Xtra*, a position I held for 13 years.) I like to think that one of the special qualities of those early columns was an openness

to failure, whether it was flailing about in the quicksand of
'90s identity politics or struggling with more quotidian dis-
appointments and confusions. I wrote without judgement,
without shame.

That lesson is essential for a writer, and much else beyond.

On one of my occasional visits to the Hassle Free Clinic
in the '90s, one of the few places back then that offered
anonymous HIV testing, the nurse asked me about my
safe sex practices. I said that I was pretty good about using
condoms for anal sex, but had slipped up a few times. "We
all slip up sometimes," she replied casually, sweetly. No
shame. That was—and remains—a crucial attitude in the
fight against HIV/AIDS. From public health and the right
to die to sex education in schools and online bullying, it's
a viewpoint critical to so many aspects of society. There's
too much indignation in the world, too much shaming, too
many secrets.

An openness to human foibles, finding joy in failure and
weakness and struggle, compassion, for myself and for others—that's what I learned at 341 Seaton Street. That is what
I strive for still in life and in writing. And I fail often. No
shame in that.

The Blitz Kid:
Falling Victim to Fashion
DEREK McCORMACK

What came first for me, fashion or faggotry?

I've always loved fashion and I've always been a faggot. I'm better at fashion than I am at being a fag—I'm never comfortable in bars or clubs and I've never been to a backroom or a bathhouse.

Boutiques are my backrooms.

The best boutiques I've been in? There was World's End in London, where I first saw a Vivienne Westwood; there was If Boutique in New York City, where I first felt a Jean-Paul Gaultier; there was the Holt Renfrew in Toronto, where I fell for an early collection by Maison Martin Margiela.

There was Seesaw. Seesaw was in Toronto; it's where I saw Blitz. Blitz wasn't a big label, but it was big for me, because Carole Pope wore it.

"With its visual flair and its peculiar brand of rock," *Maclean's* magazine said in 1982, "Rough Trade, judged both by sight and sound, is the most distinctive act in Canadian show business."

Rough Trade was founded in the 1970s, but found fame during the new wave days of the 1980s. Though the band had numerous members through the years, the core stayed

I remember Pope pretended to masturbate with her microphone stand. I remember she mock-masturbated with her hand, too, then sniffed it.

I remember she was wearing white—white baggy pants with a white unconstructed blazer. It was the same outfit she was wearing on the cover of *For Those Who Think Young*.

In the liner notes to the album, she credited her clothes to Blitz, and thanked Marilyn Kiewiet, the label's designer. In the liner notes to *Shaking the Foundations* (1982), she thanked Kiewiet again; she also thanked Seesaw, a shop that I hadn't heard of. I travelled there as soon as I was able to and bought a sweater. Blitz made it. What did it make me?

Seesaw was a shoebox of a store in a shopping arcade in the Yorkville shopping district of Toronto.

It looked like many stores I'd been in, but with better clothes. The labels were Japanese, German, Spanish. There were labels I couldn't identify.

There was Blitz. The fall/winter collection was on the racks. The sweater I picked up looked a little like the coat Carole Pope wore. It was double-breasted with a flap that came down across the front. It was black with red stripes and squiggles. It was acrylic. It was on sale: $120.

When I slipped it on I became—who? I became Carole Pope. I became Kevan Staples. I became somebody who might be in Rough Trade's world: an artist, a fashion designer, a makeup artist or hairstylist. I wanted into Rough Trade's world; I thought that *Seesaw* was a way in, I thought that a sweater was a way in, I thought that shopping was a way in. I thought: If only I have the right things to wear.

"Most of my stage clothes are made by Marilyn Kiewiet, who lives with Kevan, my partner," Carole Pope said in an interview in 1983. It was in *Limelight*, a Toronto magazine; Pope was on the cover. "I contribute ideas when I get together with Marilyn and I usually know what I want so I show her pictures and she comes up with something…I usually like everything she does."

"A more simplified trend look is the trend for the future," Kiewiet said in the same issue, in a profile of her. An American who studied fashion design in Amsterdam, she'd started Blitz in Toronto in 1980. "I want to create a look so that people will say: That's a Marilyn Kiewiet!"

Also in that issue: an ad for Seesaw.

Seesaw was magic for me. It wasn't only the store; it was the street it was on, and the streets around that street.

There were other stores on those streets that stunned me, stores where I saw the labels that Pope sang about: Fendi, Kenzo, Lagerfeld.

Yorkville, it seemed, was a song—or the setting of a song—by Rough Trade. It was a district suited to souls like me, devotees of fashion and faggotry—didn't Pope shop there? Hadn't she called it home?

Born in Britain, Pope came to Canada with her family when she was a kid. She attended high school in Scarborough—the "depths of Scarborough," as she said in her memoir, *Anti-Diva*. When she was done, she drifted downtown, to Yorkville. The city's music scene was centred there then. She played coffeehouses and bars with Kevan Staples. They called themselves O, after "The Story of O." Then they became the Bullwhip Brothers. Then, Rough Trade.

Pope was always concerned with clothes.

"Before she started earning much money, Pope shopped for striking second-hand styles at *Amelia Earhart*," the *Toronto Star* reported in 1984. "Her few designer creations were made by Sandy Stagg, who used to own and design for Amelia Earhart."

Amelia Earhart Originals was the store's full name. It started out on Charles St. W., off Yonge St.; it relocated to Yorkville Ave. after a couple of years.

Sandy Stagg specialized in stocking styles from the 1930s and 1940s; her own designs were inspired by those decades. Stagg was a doyenne of the downtown scene: what she wore and said was news. She was written up often in *FILE Megazine*, the magazine put out by General Idea. She appeared on the cover of *FILE's* glamour issue in 1975, or at least her leg did. It was wearing the Miss General Idea shoe.

Miss General Idea was a character, a conceptual caprice. General Idea created her as a parody of Miss America and other pageant glamourpusses. General Idea named shoes and dresses for her; they designed a boudoir for her; they drew up plans for a pavilion that would be built in her honour; they put on pageants in which men and women would win her title.

Staged at the Art Gallery of Ontario, the Miss General Idea Pageant of 1975 featured performances by Rough Trade. The band performed numbers they'd selected specially for the nigh. There was "I Like It, but Is It Art?" which included the lyric: "Sylvia Plath getting gassed, Warhol getting shot by Solanis, I like it, I like it, I like it, but is it art?" There was "Beauty Queen," which included the line: "You're not a drag queen or a dinge queen or a rice queen or a dairy queen…"

In 1980, General Idea had a new show at Carmen Lamanna Gallery on Yonge Street near Bloor Street W. The group exhibited Test Tube, a video work set at the Colour Bar Lounge, the fictional cocktail bar at the fictional Miss General Idea Pavilion.

In 1980, The Fiesta, a restaurant beside the Carmen Lamanna Gallery, was new. It was owned by Sandy Stagg,

who also ran Peter Pan on Queen Street West; it was deco-
rated with General Idea's art.

Avoid Freud came out that year. General Idea art directed
the album. In *Anti-Diva*, Pope reminisced about the time
she and Staples were styled by Jorge Zontal for the cover:
"Wearing Thierry Mugler suits with massive moulded
shoulder pads, with our flesh bronzed and then literally
airbrushed with makeup, we were made over into beautiful
iconic beings."

In 1980, Carole Pope was interviewed at The Fiesta.

The topic of the talk: fashion.

"Among Toronto designers," she said, "Gerald Franklin
did a great pink leather suit for me, and I have some fabulous leather outfits that were custom-made by Loucas
Kleanthous. I also adore Marilyn Kiewiet's work."

Kiewiet had started Blitz that same year. Which is not to
say that her clothes weren't known: Rough Trade wore them
onstage. Was there better publicity than Carole Pope?

After coming to Canada in 1977, Kiewiet worked for a
while at Amelia Earhart Originals, where she resewed and
reshaped vintage styles.

And: she started seeing Kevan Staples.

Almost immediately Rough Trade began appearing in
her clothes. For an appearance on Peter Gzowski's show
on CBC-TV, Pope wore a space-aged silver jumpsuit; for
another appearance on the same show, she wore a white suit
with a black striped waistcoat; for another, a black blouse
held spangled with safety pins. It portended the fashiony
punk of Stephen Sprouse.

Punk was the rage.

Pope put a shock of purple in her hair. She wore pants
with see-through plastic windows sewn into them for a seat.
She and the band performed Restless Underwear, a musical

revue co-starring Divine, at Massey Hall in Toronto. Pope was in a vinyl bondage suit.

Kiewiet was her co-conspirator, her seamstress and some-times-stylist. When Rough Trade toured, they'd take in Fiorucci and Maxfield's. In Paris, Pope and Staples and Kiewiet found Montana's leather factory and stocked up on samples. If the pieces they wanted were too pricey to purchase, Kiewiet simply made them—she had a studio, and she had skills; she'd apprenticed at a leather goods firm in Amsterdam that created coats, she said, for every gambler and gangster in town.

The clothes Kiewiet made for Rough Trade were couture; Blitz was *prêt-a-porter*.

Blitz meant that fashion-conscious souls across the country could get Carole Pope's look.

For spring and summer, there were layered cotton knits; for winter, sweaters and coats, and leather. There were primary colours and bold patterns; it was new wave, it was Memphis Group.

She showed two collections a year. She staged fashion shows in Toronto and, once, in New York; she had stockists in most major cities in the country. It was a small-scale operation: she did a few dozen looks per season, and made a few dozen copies of each look. The Blitz headquarters were in her home, but she also had an office at a factory in Toronto that manufactured her knits. And she had a position at Seesaw where she sold her own creations.

Seesaw was started by Frima Zilber in the late 1970s. By the early 1980s, Zilber was stocking Blitz, and Kiewiet was working for her at the store.

Seesaw was a perfect fit for Blitz. The store stocked knits from reasonably-priced but fashionable labels. Some of them are still remembered—Norma Kamali and Willi Smith—and some are not.

The star of the show was Kansai.

Kansai Yamamoto had been a fashion star since he showed in London in 1971. He was best known for costuming David Bowie during his Ziggy Stardust and Aladdin Sane days. When he staged runway shows in Japan, the press said, he did it in stadiums he had become a rock star himself.

Kansai's clothing had a futuristic feel, sort of sci-fi meets Hokusai: there were contemporary silhouettes with cuts that recalled kimonos; they were splashed with Japanese characters and prints of waves or tigers. Carole Pope bought a lot of it in the early 1980s. The style section of a Toronto newspaper stated that she was at risk of losing her style status if she didn't stop wearing Kansai.

I was shocked.

I was shocked by the editorial. I was shocked to think that Carole Pope wasn't fashionable.

She had been a model to me; more than fashionable, she'd seemed to be a spokesperson for fashion itself.

Then things changed. By 1984, I'd discovered Jean-Paul Gaultier; he seemed to render Montana and Mugler redundant. By 1984, I'd seen Comme des Garçons and Yohji Yamamoto's clothes in *Vogue*; they made all the clothes I'd ever seen seem redundant.

Rough Trade broke up in 1988, though it seemed as if they'd broken up before that: *O, Tempora! O, Mores!* (1984) was the band's final studio album.

Carole Pope set out performing as a solo artist. Kevan Staples set out writing music for TV and movies. Marilyn Kiewiet closed Blitz in 1984; she took time to raise her daughter, then trained as an interior designer.

Seesaw closed up sometime after that. I didn't notice. Whenever I was in Toronto, I haunted a boutique on Bloor

Street West that sold Gaultier for men. I loved the rubber-
ized shirts, the pinstripe suits with bare backs, the skirts that
were designed for men to wear. I can't recall the name of the
boutique.

It will come to me.

ONE OF THE GUYS

Steve MacIsaac

WHEN I MOVED TO THE U.S. IN 2005, I WAS SURPRISED BY HOW MANY OF MY NEW FRIENDS SAW CANADA AS A GAY MECCA.

"IT'S SO PROGRESSIVE."

"NOBODY CARES ABOUT SEXUAL ORIENTATION."

MY BULLIED INNER CHILD BALKED AT THIS.

IT CERTAINLY WASN'T MY EXPERIENCE.

I GREW UP IN RURAL NOVA SCOTIA, FAR FROM A MAJOR CITY.

MOST PEOPLE IN MY COMMUNITY WORKED WITH THEIR HANDS.

the KIDS in the HALL

FARMERS. FISHERMEN. LUMBERJACKS. TRUCK DRIVERS. MECHANICS.

ALL DRIVERS OF THE CANADIAN ECONOMIC ENGINE.

ALL ENFORCERS OF "MANLINESS."

SO HOW DID A MOSTLY RURAL NATION BASED ON TRADITIONALLY MASCULINE OCCUPATIONS BECOME ONE OF THE FIRST COUNTRIES TO LEGALIZE SAME-SEX MARRIAGE?

PERSONALLY, I THANK SCOTT THOMPSON.

THE KIDS IN THE HALL'S 1989 DEBUT WAS AN ADRENALINE SHOT INTO THE HEART OF A TELEVISION DUOPOLY SERVING UP HEAPING PORTIONS OF PLATITUDES AND PROVINCIALISM.

THEY WERE DANGEROUS. IRREVERENT. ICONOCLASTIC.

MOST IMPORTANTLY, DESPITE FOUR OUT OF THE FIVE MEMBERS BEING STRAIGHT, THEY WERE VERY, VERY QUEER.

AND THOMPSON WAS THE MOST DANGEROUS, IRREVERENT, ICONOCLASTIC, AND, YES, QUEEREST OF THEM ALL.

HIS PORTRAYAL OF GAY MEN WAS RADICAL IN 1989.

AT THE TIME GAY MEN MIGHT HAVE HAD A SWISHY BIT PART ON A SITCOM.

MAY HAVE DIED TRAGICALLY ON ONE OF THE FEW DRAMAS THAT DEIGNED TO NOTICE THE GREATEST MEDICAL CRISIS OF A GENERATION.

THOMPSON, USING HIS OWN EXPERIENCES AND THOSE OF HIS CONTEMPORARIES, BROADCAST AN UNFILTERED, UPROARIOUS PICTURE OF GAY LIFE THAT SHOCKED VIEWERES THROUGH ITS SHEER AUDACITY.

AN OUTSIZED PORTRAYAL THAT WALKED UP TO THE LINE OF CARICATURE, THOMPSON DREW THE IRE OF BOTH CONSERVATIVES, FOR DARING TO EXIST AT ALL, AND GAY PEOPLE, FOR REINFORCING "SWISHY GAY" STEREOTYPES.

KEEP IN MIND THIS WAS A SHOW TRAFFICKING IN SATANIC CABLE ACCESS PROGRAMS, HUMAN-CHICKEN HYBRIDS, AND CABBAGE-HEADED LECHES.

CHARACTERS IN SKETCH COMEDY ARE BROAD ALMOST BY DEFINITION.

WHEN YOU HAVE TO GET IN AND OUT IN FIVE MINUTES, TROPES ARE ANOTHER FORM OF SHORTHAND.

THAT BEING SAID, THE GAY THEMES THOMPSON SHARED WERE REAL, NOT "A VERY SPECIAL EPISODE," EASILY DIGESTED AND JUST AS EASILY FORGOTTEN.

AS MANY BULLIED SCHOOLCHILDREN KNOW, ONE SUREFIRE WAY TO GET THE BULLIES OFF YOUR BACK IS TO BE THE FUNNIEST MOTHERFUCKER IN THE ROOM.

THE FARMERS, FISHERMEN, LUMBERJACKS, MECHANICS AND TRUCK DRIVERS WHO WOULD HAVE BEEN KICKING THOMPSON'S ASS IF THEY RAN INTO HIM AT A BAR WERE INSTEAD LAUGHING WITH HIM ON A WEEKLY BASIS.

FOR MANY CANADIANS, THIS MAY HAVE BEEN THE FIRST POSITIVE PORTRAYAL OF A GAY MAN THEY HAD SEEN ON TV.

IT MOST CERTAINLY WAS MINE.

MORE IMPORTANTLY, DESPITE BEING SO VISIBLY AND MEMORABLY "OUT," HE WAS A COMEDIAN FIRST.

HE WASN'T A QUEER MINSTREL ONLY TROTTED OUT TO PROP UP NUMBERS WITH DRAG OR CAMP.

HE WAS JUST ONE OF THE GUYS.

IN SOME ASPECTS HE WAS THE MOST VERSATILE MEMBER OF THE TROUPE.

IN TOTO, HE PLAYED CONVENTIONAL ROLES, SUCH AS DADS AND BUSINESSMEN, FAR MORE FREQUENTLY THAN GAY ONES.

HE WAS THE ONLY CAST MEMBER WHO COULD PLAY A THUG CONVINCINGLY.

HE PLAYED A WOMANIZER MORE THAN ONCE.

A FERAL SEXUALITY PUSHING THROUGH, WHETHER PLAYING STRAIGHT OR GAY.

THOMPSON CONSISTENTLY PUSHED AGAINST THE LIMITS OF CBC NETWORK CENSORSHIP.

REFUSING TO CONFORM TO TV'S NEUTERED, ASEXUAL REPRESENTATION OF GAY MEN.

THE OTHER MEMBERS WERE ALSO GAME, ALL OF THEM PLAYING GAY AT ONE POINT OR ANOTHER.

THOMPSON WAS NOT A LONE VOICE, BUT ONE OF FIVE MEN WITH THE CONFIDENCE TO PLAY WITH GENDER REPRESENTATION.

ALL OF THEM DID UTTERLY CONVINCING DRAG.

MORE THAN ONE HETEROSEXUAL MALE HAS BEEN SEXUALLY CONFUSED BY SEEING A CAST MEMBER IN A DRESS.

KIDS' MEMBER MARC MCKINNEY HAS STATED THAT THOMPSON "HAD A BIG INFLUENCE ON THE WAY WE PLAYED WOMEN, WHICH IS: IT'S NOT A COMMENT... WE'RE JUST GOING TO PLAY IT STRAIGHT."

THAT SAME ESSENTIAL HUMANITY ALSO PERMEATED HOW THEY PORTRAYED GAY.

115

EVERY WEEK FOR FIVE YEARS, CANADA WAS INTRODUCED TO AN ALTERNATE UNIVERSE.

ONE IN WHICH STRICT BOUNDARIES BETWEEN STRAIGHT AND GAY, MALE AND FEMALE WERE CONSTANTLY BLURRED.

A UNIVERSE WHERE GAY MARRIAGE WOULDN'T HAVE BEEN A STRETCH.

THOMPSON'S GONE ON THE RECORD AS NOT BEING ESPECIALLY ENTHUSIASTIC ABOUT THAT TOPIC.

THIS WHOLE MARRIAGE THING

I MEAN, I UNDERSTAND IT AND I'M FOR IT

BUT MY HEART ISN'T IN IT.

FOR MY GENERATION, IT WAS JUST STAYING ALIVE.

AN ENTIRE GENERATION SAW BEING GAY AS NO BIG DEAL.

YOU'RE FIRED

AS A CONFUSED YOUNG MAN WHO ROUTINELY LIED TO MAKE THINGS EASY

FOR OTHERS, AND FOR MYSELF

THOMPSON'S WEEKLY REFUSAL TO MAKE THINGS COMFORTABLE HIT HOME.

EXIT

HE SHOWED ME THE IMPORTANCE OF HONESTY

OF NOT ASKING PERMISSION

IN AN ERA OF FORCED INVISIBILITY, SCOTT THOMPSON FORCED PEOPLE TO LOOK

MADE GAY LIFE SALIENT

A RADICAL ACT OF NORMALCY.

Permission

NANCY JO CULLEN

In grade twelve I discovered an ad in *The Kelowna Daily Courier*. The Theatre Arts program at David Thompson University Centre in Nelson BC (a place I knew only as the home for our region's Bishop) was holding auditions. I made a madcap road trip there with two high-school buddies, in a beat up old VW that took the Selkirk Mountain ascents at about twenty kilometres an hour. We stayed in a scruffy hotel and while underage we snuck into a bar and got hammered. A few months later I moved to Nelson.

Nelson is located in the Selkirk Mountains on the far west arm of Kootney Lake in the traditional territory of the Ktunaxa and Sinixt peoples. Even before the restoration of its downtown heritage buildings in the mid-1980s, it was a beautiful town built on and between steep hills. It is populated with charming Victorian architecture including the City Hall and post office, which were designed by the British architect Francis Rattenbury. The West Kootneys were a more rugged region than the Okanagan home to Kelowna, and Nelson, although considerably smaller than my home-town, was years ahead and surprisingly progressive.

When I arrived in Nelson from the Okanagan Valley in September 1980 I was eighteen and embarking on a two-year Theatre Arts diploma at David Thompson University

Centre, an art school on the campus of the former Catholic University Notre Dame. Although only a four-hour drive from the Okanagan, Nelson, with its preponderance of hippies, draft-dodgers, and visible homosexuals, was a world away from my hometown. Kelowna, alternatively, seemed to have a disproportionately high number of rich people and bible thumpers. It was the home to Social Credit leader and BC Premier, Bill Bennett, who was inspired by the thinking of Milton Friedman (advisor to both Ronald Reagan and Margaret Thatcher). Kelowna was a four seasons playground, a great place for recreational sports and summer vacations but not necessarily the best spot for a kid who felt different but couldn't yet articulate what that difference was about.

So, Nelson was a fortunate place for me to land. It would take another decade for me to come out, but the two years I spent in Nelson did all the things a couple of years in college should do. Those years allowed me to party, to get laid a few times, to fall in love with a boy, to experiment with LSD, and most importantly, I witnessed a small but vibrant community of queer folk getting on with their lives.

Up until Nelson, my knowledge of the LGBTQ world was limited. Growing up I knew of a couple of gay men who lived very quietly not exactly out, not exactly closeted. When I was thirteen I'd read a salacious article in *Cosmo* that "documented" an affair between a married woman and her visiting friend, and when I was seventeen I devoured the novel *Kinflicks* by Lisa Alther. I had an idea that women could be lesbians but (although girls loving girls seemed an excellent thing) I was a Catholic daughter. This meant that while bad behaviour was to be expected at times, there was really only so far a good Catholic could go. In my Catholic upbringing there were two kinds of sin; there was the kind of sin a mother could abide (getting drunk, smoking weed, getting knocked up out of wedlock) and then there was SIN, the kind that brought on a mother's perpetual silence and all eternity burning in hell (committing murder or becoming a lesbian). It didn't matter what my rational mind understood, my Catholic indoctrination overrode any sensible response to my own desire and curiosity. Catholic programming was like an antibiotic-resistant infection that once it had its grip on you was nearly impossible to shake off. I simply put the thought out of my head.

So, Nelson was a revelation. It was a small town with a large, thriving queer community. And queer people lived in Nelson as though it was their perfect right to be there: to eat, and sleep, and work, and even to take roles in the local college's theatre productions. This was, for me, infinitely daring, that claiming of space, without asking or waiting for permission from some authority that was hardly likely to offer it anyway. And, in retrospect, it was daring that thirty-five years ago a small community of queers lived so openly in a relatively isolated place, far from international airports and large, cultured urban centres.

First-year students in the Theatre Arts program at DTUC were required to build the sets for each of the six productions we staged during the school year. This meant that any time not spent in class or rehearsal was spent constructing sets. We worked our asses off and spent an inordinate amount of time in one another's company. One of our company was Kate Johnston, the first out lesbian I ever met. To my eighteen-year-old eyes, Kate was the quintessential worldly woman; twenty-six years old and living off campus with her girlfriend and her girlfriend's dog, Nookie.

Kate was at ease in the world. She was easy to talk to, comfortable sharing tidbits about her life while also dishing about politics, feminism and queer rights. She was kind and non-judgemental. And I was a little bit in awe of Kate, with her dashing swagger and wild, curly hair. She was a rich and sometimes racy wellspring of information and insight.

From Kate I learned the meaning of nookie, aha! not some endearing name for a dog who liked small spaces as I might have imagined, but rather slang for fucking. (It's not that I arrived at DTUC a complete innocent, but the term was new to me.) I also learned from Kate that Nelson was home to the third largest per-capita queer community in North America, outside of San Francisco. And Kate was the first to present me with the appalling statistics regarding roles for women in theatre as opposed to roles for men. The numbers were shocking; something like for every seven roles created for men one role was created for women, and our little theatre program was not doing any better than the statistical norm.

Like me, Kate came from a large Irish-Catholic family but she did not appear to be suffering from shame, my psychic thumbscrew. Kate was just Kate; she could hardly be described as confrontational but she sure as hell wasn't waiting around for anyone's permission to be her authentic self. In our second year at theatre school the roles for female students had increased remarkably. I wasn't the only person Kate talked to about the opportunities for roles for women in a program we were all paying equally for.

I should say that I am a gender normative woman, female assigned and female at birth. And so being queer, looking queer initially felt like it had an element of choice. The desire for approval and my struggle to come out, were attached to my willingness (or rather, lack thereof) to let go of the privileges attached to hetero-normative behaviour. To put it very simply, I was distressed by the idea that people, particularly my parents, wouldn't like me anymore.

I am the last child of seven. I grew up in mostly happy chaos with parents whose child-rearing style would best be described as: you made your bed, you lie in it. Jokes were an important part of my family's culture, as was booze. Making my mom laugh was good, pissing her off or making her cry was bad. Pulling up your socks and soldiering on, keeping up a good front was very, very important. All of this is to say that while fighting over the last pack of Dad's Cookies might have been an acceptable form of confrontation, a high value was placed on being likeable, and, ultimately, being likeable involved conforming to a hetero-normative status quo; opposite sex partners, babies, and showing up for work no matter how hungover you were. And no one really wanted to make my mom angry, her silence could be deafening and last for days. In the case of my coming out, I feared it would last for years.

Of course, I'm hardly the first queer person who has found themselves in such a quandary. And maybe after the fact, in the telling, our stories sound very similar, but how and when and where we come out is an intensely personal process muddled by our upbringings and close relationships. I have an inner keener and she buys into that idea that there is a right way and a wrong way to do things. Sometimes that inner keener makes me feel I did it wrong; my coming out should have been faster or braver. Sometimes, after twenty-five years of being out I still wonder why I couldn't do it sooner, why I couldn't have been a better queer. It is that kind of thinking that brings to mind the memory of Anthony Jones.

For its musical productions, the theatre department at DTUC employed the services of a musical director from the town of Nelson. And so, in my first year, in addition to spending a great deal of time with Kate, I also spent a significant portion of my time in the company of Anthony Jones, a fifty-something, white-haired, plump, outrageously gay man. I had been cast in the role of the eponymous heroine in the musical production of Irma la Douce. Let me just say, I was ill-cast, barely able to carry a tune with absolutely no dancing experience save for that year of ballet that ended with me flunking my first and only dance exam about ten years previous, but I was around the right height and weight for the director's idea of the role and I nailed my rendition of Silent Night at the audition. It's laughable now but I was excited about it then, even if I was the only woman in the entire program with a role in that play.

Anthony Jones had a British accent, was limp wristed, smoked cigarettes, drank Scotch and delighted in driving a Ram (get it?) Charger. I don't remember much of the content of our conversations, however I do remember feeling a prudish shock at many of his observations and anecdotes. He was, as the haters today might say, in your face. He was also kind and generous and spent hours coaching me in the basics of carrying a tune. It wasn't exactly a futile task but it could hardly have been rewarding. Still, I bet he had a not unkind giggle over the review that compared my voice to a rusty hinge because it was fair, and funny.

Anthony had a story too, but he died of esophageal cancer in 1990 and my nineteen-year-old self didn't think to ask him about his story in 1981. But I know this much: Anthony had been previously married and had two daughters, younger than me, in their early teens if memory serves me correctly, and they lived in another city. I believe if Anthony had lived he'd be in his mid-eighties, so he would have come of age in a time and place where the pressure for him to conform to heterosexual norms would have been great. What route his path took I'll never know but he was out and loud when we met one another. If, for me, Kate Johnston exemplified the path of the fierce, young queer, Anthony Jones was no less fiercely queer in his mid life. Perhaps what I learned from Anthony is that you get there when you do and when you arrive make sure as hell you're having a good time.

Nevertheless, Kate became a beacon of sorts in my life. When theatre school ended we had no reason to keep in touch and we didn't, but the closer I came to coming out, the more I thought about young Kate, (out since late adolescence and still close to her family!) She was doing her thing; keeping it real. If Kate could do it with her bounty of sisters and her Roman Catholic parents, surely I could too, surely my family could as well?

When I finally came out to my mom in 1992 (my dad had been dead ten years by then), she didn't cry, but man, was she pissed off. I remember leaving her tiny apartment and driving across town in a daze. I said to my then partner never tell your mom. We had both been planning to tell our Catholic mothers the whole truth so that we could live authentically. It's not worth it! I cried. But my mom called me three days after she lost her shit on me and apologized for her lousy attitude; it didn't take her years as I had feared. It turns out the Johnstons weren't the only Roman Catholic family who could love their queer members, but I'm grateful that Kate and her family provided a positive example of what the outcome with my own family could be.

In the ensuing years between theatre school and reconnecting with her on Facebook, I often thought about Kate, who I knew to be living and working in theatre in Toronto. It's not easy to continually struggle to make ends meet and many of our cohorts went on to more stable work, but Kate persisted in the creative life. Throughout the past few decades she has worked in theatre and film collaborating on feminist/lesbian/queer work, including projects with trans activist and playwright Alec Butler.

When Kate was planning her move into filmmaking and began to study script writing and production she understood that if she was going to tell the stories she wanted, then she would have to make the films on her own, or with other women or queer filmmakers. Thirty-five years ago, when we were both much younger, Kate was already talking about strong women, and creating work with strong female characters. She's still at it, and in 2014 she released her first full-length feature, *Tru Love*. In an industry that's disinclined to support female and/or queer filmmakers, Kate is (still) not waiting for permission to do her thing.

When I finally came out at the age of 30, when my comfort became more important than my mother's comfort, attitudes, at least in Canada, were changing. I owe a debt to Kate and Anthony and to people like them, who didn't fight (or stopped fighting) their essential selves; who lived openly and happily and didn't wait for permission from some outside source to live their authentic lives.

I spent a lot of my teens and twenties worrying about the prospect of hell and working through my beliefs with respect to God, free will and sin (cue scary music). If the paradigm of right/wrong or good/bad entered into things then surely it was answered by my fortuitous discovery of Nelson; I didn't seek out Nelson because I knew about the queers and the draft dodgers and hippies, I sought out Nelson because it was conveniently close to home. And moving to Nelson brought with it friendship with Kate and lessons gleaned from Anthony. (Sing! Sing out loud!) If there was some deity in the sky overseeing the course of my days then why was I led to a town lit up by queer folk?

In 1982 I left Nelson knowing that I wanted to have the kind of life I witnessed there; the kind of lives Kate and Anthony were living. It took me ten more years to get there, but I am grateful for the excellent good luck that landed me in one of the loveliest places I'd ever been, peopled by characters who filled me with inspiration to lead the life that felt most natural to me.

Paul Baker: an ~~an~~ introduction

September 1982: First Year Registration Day at the Ontario College of Art. Despite the chaos and confusion, a feeling of excitement was palpable. And yet, something wasn't quite right.

I'd been to a few OCA Open Houses with my sister in the past, and cherished the memory of one student's outlandish getup.

EXPERIMENTAL   LIBERAL ARTS   GENERALS

Fun-fur Kleenex box cover

Inflatable alligator strapped to chest.

Maurice Vellekoop

I'd expected everyone at art school would be equally outrageous.

These people look just like the people in **high** school.

Where are all the weirdos? How are you supposed to meet anyone... like you?

Wait, look!

Over there!

Uh, I love what you're wearing!

Thanks. Are you as confused as me? It seems to me all we **really** have to do is register for one elective. Sound right?

Uh-huh.

Which were you thinking of?

I'm very interested in this "Plays in Performance."

Me too! I think that's the lineup over there.

C'mon, they're filling up fast.

Wow, check her out! Now that's what an art student looks like!

We **have** to talk to her.

As the first weeks of art school went by, my initial impression only worsened. My new friend Deirdre was the only sophisticated person I'd met.

Listen to this.

We got an assignment to do a drawing in the style of Beardsley. So this girl comes to class this week and says, "I couldn't find a book on **Aud**rey Beardsley anywhere."

Oh my God.

I realized not everyone had been lucky enough to grow up in an art library like my house, but **still**.

What about the plastic fruit in the still life we had to paint in 'Media'?

Puh-leeze!

From the start, "Plays in Performance" was different, an oasis of intellectual stimulation.

... and a quick reminder Wednesday, we'll be meeting at the Tarragon Theatre for our next student discount subscription, Ibsen's "The Master Builder." Oh my.

The instructor was an incredibly tall, intimidatingly smart, wickedly funny, **very** out gay man.

So today I'm flinging you all right into the deep end with "King Lear," Shakespeare's late, dark fairy tale tragedy.

The film was adapted by Peter Brook from a Royal Shakespeare Company production starring Paul Scofield. Brook was famous for a legendary staging of "A Midsummer Night's Dream" that took place entirely inside a giant white box.

I was entranced. Each week, Paul produced some miraculous fresh wonder: a documentary on Martha Graham,

I'm wearing my hair as Jocasta, or at least as I hope she wore it.

Laurence Olivier's film of "Three Sisters," designed by Josef Svoboda, and starring the divine Joan Plowright as Masha,

To our jolly life, come what may!

Tyrone Guthrie's Stratford, Ontario production of "Oedipus Rex," with masks by Tanya Moiseiwitsch.

Whoever among you knows by what man Laius, son of Labdacus, was killed, must **tell all he knows**.

Once, the life-changing films of Kenneth Anger!

"Plays in Performance" was not so much an introductory exploration of theatre art.

What we were **really** getting...

As a footnote to our previous discussion, I thought I'd play the 'blasted heath' scene from Aribert Reiman's opera of "King Lear."

131

... was a window onto the myriad, sui generis obsessions,

Plink TINKLE Plunk CRASH! BOOM! GROAN

AV LOANS

The brilliant, never pretentious opinions,

Alright, so it wasn't "The Boogie-woogie Bugle Boy of Company B!"

AV LOANS

and iconic catch-phrases,

More misogyny!

Freudian field day!

of its creator, Doctor Paul Baker.

That's it for today. See you at the theatre!

"QUITTIN' TIME!"

I'se da boss here at Tara. I'se da one who says when it's quittin' time. **QUITTIN' TIME!**

How did you **know** that?

He just knows.

In that moment, Paul and I became instant friends,

and from then on, most of our conversations consisted of dialogue from old movies ...

Just a minute now.

Doctor Sugar...

Katharine Hepburn! "Suddenly Last Summer!"

I want those lies *CUT* out of her brain.

... and - they - were - **EATING HIM!!**

HA HA HA HA HA!

Liz Taylor is so awful, isn't she?

Oh, I don't know. She was a great supporter of Tennessee Williams.

Really?

I was at a Williams conference once, where she spoke quite movingly about him. She even gave a very affecting reading.

133

L-l-l-little did they r-r-r-realize how much I enjoyed being m-m-m-manhandled by those meaty boys!

What was **that**?

Anthony Blanche. You know, from "Brideshead Revisited?" That series?

In high school, me and my friends were **obsessed** with it. Each week we'd excitedly review the latest episode.

I'm jealous. There was nothing like that when I was your age.

Hmm.

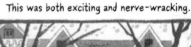

Most of the time, the nearly twenty-year age difference was irrelevant, non-existent. We just... clicked.

The following spring, Paul invited me to his house in Cabbagetown for dinner with him and his partner.

This was both exciting and nerve-wracking.

I'd met Martin a few times at theatrical outings.

Can we give you a lift to the subway?

That would be great!

He rarely spoke and was a somewhat intimidating presence.

How awkward was this going to be?

Oh, hi Maurice. Paul isn't here.

Oh? Sorry, I'm early. Should I... come back later?

Don't be silly. Come on in.

I brought some wine I hope it's okay?

Thanks. Would you like some? A beer?

Um, beer would be great.

135

Excuse me. I'm going to go get changed. Make yourself at home.

What were you **thinking**? **No**body arrives **early**.

It'll get better when Paul arrives. You'll see!

=SLAM=

FUCK! SHIT!

That **fucking** market! They were out of **coriander**!

137

Martin warmed up considerably, displaying a sly, dry English wit. I would come to realize, he was actually kind of shy.

What ever did we talk about? I was too busy soaking up the sophisticated atmosphere to remember.

One thing is certain: just as on the hundreds of similar evenings that would follow, there was music.

Acerba volutta, dolce torturo

Paul had a PhD in English Literature, had taught film at Western University, and clearly knew all there was to know about the stage, but his greatest love was opera.

lentissima agonia, rapida offesa

Paul shopped for records daily, ever on the lookout for some fresh, undiscovered, singing sensation.

Vampa, gelo, tremor, smania, paura, ad amoroso, sen

My own opera obsession, a direct result of our friendship, would have to wait another year or two. Opera was too redolent of my Dad, whom I'd vowed never to emulate in any way.

torna l'attesa

138

Later, we most certainly watched some treasure from Paul's vast collection of arcanely labeled video-tapes, decipherable only to him - if he was lucky.

Just a minute now...

Was it "Shanghai Express?" "Female Trouble?" A particularly juicy scene from his beloved "All My Children?"

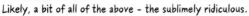

Likely, a bit of all of the above - the sublimely ridiculous.

Well, I better scoot, before the subway shuts down. Thank you. This was... incredible!

Get home safe now, hear?

Yes, be careful on those streets.

I will, good night!

You found them! The weirdos!

Yeah, people like you, at last!

139

General Idea and Me:
Unfulfilled Expectations
NIK SHEEHAN

My most profound experience with the art of General Idea came in 1991 during a viewing of their *Fin de Siècle* installation at the Power Plant, on Toronto's waterfront. In one brightly lit gallery, Styrofoam sheets were arranged as broken ice floes, on which lay three plaintive-looking white baby harp seals. The peacefulness of the tableau and the cool calm of the display affected me profoundly, as only art can. It was immensely healing. The ice floes resembled broken ziggurats, like the outlandish outfits worn by Miss General Idea in the 1970s. The baby seals had replaced the iconic poodles that sealed their fame and fortune in the mid '80s. Now, the members of GI were stranded on ice floes in the guise of doe-eyed seal pups. One Year of AZT/One Day of AZT—consisting of enormous coloured pills representing an early, unsuccessful treatment for AIDS—filled the other gallery. It was known that two members of GI had contracted the disease. Parody, irony, helplessness; the giant pills and the baby seals were a thudding reminder of our corporeal selves, our "soft machines," to use W.S. Burroughs' memorable phrase.

Typical of GI's method, the gift shop offered affordable art you could take home in the form of small replica harp seals made of soap. It was deep whimsy: frightening, sad, brilliant.

To explain why *Fin de Siècle* was so personally affecting, I need to tell you about General Idea and me, which is a GI notion. It's a mirror they hold up. Another GI concept you should know about, also associated with Toronto, is unfulfilled expectations.

I became aware of General Idea thirteen years earlier, as a teenager buying *The Body Politic* at a store in the Westgate Shopping Centre in Ottawa, one of those nondescript mini malls typical of suburban North America. It was the late 1970s, perhaps the Western world's most fertile artistic period to date. The hippie buzz of the sixties had penetrated deep into the mainstream. Hollywood was turning out sophisticated originals like *Tommy* and *Apocalypse Now*. It was a time when mall bookstores sold the *Joy of Sex* and the *Joy of Gay Sex*. Rock music was at its zenith, much still heard today: Led Zeppelin, Pink Floyd, Elton John, local faves Rush and Supertramp. The Sex Pistols were breaking big. John Lennon was still alive.

The sticky green Moroccan hashish widely available in suburban Ottawa was cheap and would come to your door via a fuzzy-lipped teenager, but you had to go out and find your own porn, especially gay porn. So I'd buy copies of *The Body Politic* and *Super-8 Film-maker*, slip *Numbers* underneath, gratefully acknowledge the sales clerks' indifference, then race to my Toyota to look at naked men and marvel at worlds unknown.

The Body Politic got read last. It was the depressing part of being gay, the part that said you had to fight for your right to be a real member of society. Founded as a collective, like General Idea, it became Pink Triangle Press, today's mainstream gay Canadian publisher, and I'd eventually write for them. By 1979 it was the most controversial magazine in Canada, having been raided by the police the previous year after the publication of Gerald Hannon's catalytic, still controversial article "Men Loving Boys Loving Men," a journalistic portrait of a group of pedophiles.

On one visit to the store, *FILE* magazine was there. It was the *Trangressions* issue of 1979. The cover featured a blond young man holding a glass of milk and sporting a white Hitler moustache, with the cheeky title "Nazi Milk," anticipating by two decades the ironic "Hipster Hitler" art of the twenty-first century, to say nothing of ideas of transgression. Flipping through it, I was transfixed. The three artists who created it had a "glamour" manifesto and called themselves General Idea, like a rock band. Loaded with sardonic and witty juxtapositions, it was smart, it was edgy, and it was from Toronto.

World-class Montreal had Leonard Cohen, great (French) homegrown cinema and a cosmopolitan culture even today superior to Toronto's. Because of Pierre Trudeau's over-reaching War Measures Act of 1971, a generation turned against the federal government and the Quebec nationalists took power in 1976, effectively shutting down Montreal as a desirable destination for Anglos looking for a life in the arts. Toronto, where to this day you will hear the plaintive demand it be regarded as "world class," was the only big city available (Vancouver didn't come online until the twenty-first century). That something as ingenious as General Idea could emerge from the dour homeland of Presbyterian Canada was a little bit astounding. Even better, by the early eighties, other creative noises were coming out of the place—Max Webster, Klaatu, Martha and the Muffins. In 1980, none other than General Idea art-directed the cover for Rough Trade's *Avoid Freud*, featuring uberdyke

Carole Pope in nifty shoulder pads singing of her lust for schoolgirls. Was Toronto actually, possibly hip?

AA Bronson, born Michael Tims in Vancouver in 1944, has often spoken of his delight subverting the Toronto zeitgeist. Felix Partz, born Ronald Gabe in 1945, was from Winnipeg, and Jorge Zontal (as in "horizontal"), nee Siobodan Saia-Lvey, was born in Parma, Italy in 1944. They came together as part of the youth culture flowering in the late 60s. Though formed on the concept of a rock band, General Idea never used this iconography in their art. The collective started with a larger group and ended up with the three most committed members, but instead of a commune they were more a boutique. They wanted to be in the business district.

Blending gallery and store by selling pieces of the art— what they called "multiples"—was a key idea from the beginning. But the idea of saleable works in the gallery would have a difficult time transferring to museums. It led to conflicts with the gift shop. The Museum of Modern Art insisted on hiding the multiples under Plexiglas, thus negating the point of the art at the same time GI made theirs.

Ever clever, they were soon putting reflective blinds on their art dealer Carmine Lamanna's storefront, so that passersby could be their own art works. The playfulness of the Miss General Idea Pavilions, fashion shows of the future held in unusual venues like the atrium of the Art Gallery of Ontario fused performance art, camp, artifice and design. When the three tired of it, they staged first a destruction, and then an archeological dig to retrieve lost treasures. Some of this was imaginary and fantastical, in recognition of the emptiness of hype. Your expectations might be unfulfilled.

Conceptual artists, they began with mail art, developed performance art and installations—highlighted by the *Miss*

General Idea Pageants—embraced video, and published and widely distributed the large format zine-like magazine *FILE,* from 1972–89, itself a work of art. The poodles—various images of poodles or themselves as "poodles of the art world"—defined their image in the 80s and proved their most popular series. Though they were wide-ranging in style, their many works were nearly always identifiable. Whether due to the sharp intelligence, the humour, or even the edge, GI was the height of Canadian sophistication.

They only rarely worked in traditional line drawing, but the craft was always impeccable. Never did the mask slip, or perhaps, as they suggested, theirs was a mirror rather than a mask. While they were consummate scenesters, the art was unabashedly cerebral, drawing on the sages of postwar philosophy. There was Susan Sontag's 1964 essay "Notes on Camp," with its manifesto-like evocation of apolitical and ironic appreciation for all things kitsch. In the same year, Marshall McLuhan's *Understanding Media* startled people by saying we should look at the media itself, not what's on it. Roland Barthes' *Mythologies* (1957), with its analysis of how myths reinforce the status quo, and W.S. Burroughs' saurian insights kept GI firmly wedged in the radical art tradition, with a dose of Gertrude Stein's just-so sense of irony. Andy Warhol, an obvious influence, was an early subscriber to *FILE* and began publishing his simulacrum *Interview* magazine soon after.

Famously, GI was sued by the Time-LIFE Corporation in 1976 for copyright infringement due to the similarity of the typeface and design of *FILE* with *LIFE* magazine. Ridicule by Robert Hughes in the *Village Voice* brought an end to the lawsuit, and GI changed the typeface slightly, but copyright and its meaning would run through much of their art, reaching a kind of apex with the appropriation of Robert Indiana's LOVE poster in 1987.

GI lasted 25 years, the first two decades in Toronto, with a foray to New York until they came back to Toronto to die. They attracted an appreciative following internationally and were collected by the finer institutions. Exhibitions have continued. There was a major retrospective in 2011. *FILE* has been reprinted in a boxed set. Toronto's Art Metropole, which GI founded in 1974 as an archive and publisher for contemporary art, is a going concern today. In November of 2014, curator Philip Monk, a long-time fan, included the Miss General Idea Pavilion in his show *Is Toronto Burning?* at the York University art gallery, prompting Murray Whyte, art critic of the *Toronto Star,* to opine that with the addition of Michael Snow, GI was the most bona fide art movement out of Toronto since the Group of Seven.

Yet despite wide agreement about GI's place in the pantheon, they remained just offstage. The fact is, General Idea made art for smart people. Even *FILE* couldn't be called populist.

As every artist must, GI rode the waves of fashion, and their late '80s embrace of camp, glamour and facade was a shining moment, but they were always transgressive. They could hardly sell out when the whole point of the exercise was to be rich and glamorous. The words from the first *FILE* magazine remained their manifesto to the end: "We wanted to be famous, glamorous, and rich. That is to say, we wanted to be artists and we knew that if we were famous and glamorous we could say we were artists and we would be…We did and we are. We are famous, glamorous artists."

They avoided being "politically" gay—camp calls for an apolitical stance—though just as with the Beats—Ginsberg, Burroughs and whatever Kerouac was—it was clear enough to anyone who wanted to investigate that these were queer folk.

GI's brilliant 1986 video *Shut the Fuck Up* (on YouTube and well worth Googling) blends an episode of the camp TV classic *Batman* with dancing poodles, followed by another manifesto, of sorts. The message to those who would categorize and analyze them is clear. The three of them take turns: "That's us...we know how to live and we know how to please. What pleases the media? An artist in artist drag. Even if you're not in drag, they find a way to dress you up, before they dress you down. If you complain, they've got you typecast. It's a waste of time telling the media to...shut the fuck up!"

Their work transcended identity politics, until AIDS.

I slammed into Toronto mostly unprepared late in 1982, haunting the Cameron House art bar on Queen Street wearing overalls I'd painted with cosmic symbols. I wrote for *NOW Magazine*, the hip new weekly. The exciting *Chromaliving Show* in 1984 was my first cover story. Painting and sculpture, the old thing, were the new thing. The sprawling group show was held in a converted department store in the Colonnade on Bloor Street, where GI occupied the penthouse suite above the fray.

I was out so I was the writer for gay stories. I wasn't keen on being the "gay reporter," but I played the role. Identity politics involves too much thought control, and as any minority knows, it's absurd to think anyone can represent everybody in a given population. But being publicly out meant something important. Homophobia, like all bigotry, is ridiculous, when it isn't deadly. The Toronto Police actually smashed down bathhouse doors in 1981, arresting all the inhabitants, costing the legal system millions and causing untold trauma. Court cases stretched well into the 1980s. Most of us knew someone who had been gay-bashed.

My first AIDS story, and the first for *NOW Magazine*, was advice from the Red Cross for gay men to please not donate blood. The face of the story was Peter, a winsome blond just diagnosed. He kept repeating: "I have no intention of dying."

I wrote Peter's obit a few weeks later. So began the process of visiting hospitals and hospices, holding hands, attending funerals, consoling parents and waiting for signs of infection in myself, all the while dabbing Liquid Paper to erase the names that once filled my address book. In a real war everyone shares the pain of loss. In this epidemic, people wanted to turn away, and it was understandable. Homosexual desire could kill, horribly, all due to one unguarded moment. My friend Tyler B. dropped ecstasy and checked out the bathhouse. George K. got infected the first time he had sex. When it got to be too much, I was sent to a psychiatrist, Stephen W., who diagnosed my AIDS paranoia as not being out to my parents, curing me instantly. A few months later I read of Stephen's death from AIDS. It was relentless.

The enemies of tolerance smugly smirked. Susan Sontag had revamped her essay *Illness as Metaphor* for the AIDS era, in which she argued, with brave futility, that illness was not metaphor at all. We used the cover image from her original book, a man with a serpent wrapped around his arm, for a flyer at the premiere of *No Sad Songs*, the film I made under the auspices of the AIDS Committee of Toronto in 1985. Everyone saw AIDS as metaphor.

Toronto is famously parochial, it's not big enough for scenes to inter-lap till they blur. There were always grumblings among the gay activists that GI weren't open, or out enough, with their sexuality. (This about three men who painted themselves as three poodles fucking.) As such, the initial reaction to their most iconic work, the AIDS poster, was puzzlement, hurt and hostility.

In 1987, in response to a request for a piece of an AIDS benefit, GI came up with a wry manipulation of Robert Indiana's ubiquitous "LOVE" logo by arranging the four letters of "AIDS" in the same colourful way. They soon expanded on the idea, mass printing posters. It was a powerful provocation. Indiana, himself a gay man, expressed concern, objecting to the typographical "D" (admittedly, a fair criticism). Unlike the *LIFE* magazine logo, the Indiana LOVE original had shown up so frequently its copyright couldn't be enforced. Activists were horrified. To equate AIDS with love was perverse, at best. Irony and AIDS were startling bedfellows. Yet there could be no mistaking the anger it expressed.

The AIDS poster would be associated with GI to the end, appearing in many permutations, all part of *The AIDS Project*, which would consume them until the deaths of Zontal and Partz in 1994. With the poster, here was a literal interpretation of Burroughs' concept of the word as a virus. They presented it printed multiple times in a variety of public spaces in major cities, from Times Square billboards to the sides of trams in Amsterdam. Pre-Internet, they wanted it to go viral. It was more agitprop than the seals and pills of *Fin de Siècle*, and not at all subtle—but neither was AIDS, but then AIDS ruined everything.

There was a final, posthumous gallery show for General Idea. *Infections*, in 1995, featured the AIDS poster as wallpaper, along with reproduced Mondrian paintings that GI had "infected" with dabs of green paint, because Mondrian loathed green. It was clever and sly but depressing and a little bit nauseating.

I interviewed survivor AA Bronson for *Xtra!* that June for a cover story on GI to mark the final show. Nearly 50, he was sporting the same long beard he has today. Soft-spoken and palpably depressed, he told me how their penthouse had become a hospice for Jorge and Felix, that Jorge delighted in writing cheques to friends in lieu of a will, and that Felix bitterly focused on creating new works. The death photos of Jorge were elaborately staged and would stare out from gallery walls for decades to come. Bronson said that from a financial point of view, they should have made more poodle pictures. Amusingly, he provided *Xtra!* with pictures of himself as young and clean-shaven for the cover story.

Fifteen years after picking up *FILE* in the Westgate Mall, I was talking to a member of General Idea, and we were mutually surrounded by unfulfilled expectations. Survivor guilt is painful, its own form of post-traumatic stress disorder. I was feeling it, I sensed he was too. The resulting story, aiming to be upbeat, stressed GI's success, though this was all about art about AIDS. I doubt many people read it. I was never happy about the article; I wanted GI to be fabulous forever, not stranded on an ice floe, or punking Mondrian.

In the catalogue for the retrospective held in Paris and Toronto in 2011, Bronson explained GI's method with a Burroughsian metaphor: "Our ability to live and act in contradiction defined our work: we were similarly fascinated and repulsed by the mechanisms of today's cultural economy. We injected ourselves into the mainstream of this infectious culture and lived as parasites off our monstrous host."

Bronson has done admirably well on his own. His work has been preoccupied with spiritualism since the deaths of his colleagues, he has dabbled in the occult arts. He pioneered the New York art book fair, with typical foresight promoting the popularity of books as objects. He was in the news in 2010 when he demanded the return of his portrait of Jorge Zontal from an exhibition on AIDS portraits in the

National Portrait Gallery in Washington. He nobly objected to censorship in the form of the removal of a sacrilegious video from the same show at the behest of a right-wing interest group. Despite backing from the National Gallery of Canada, his request was denied, but he made his point. *The New York Times* carried the story. Again there is prescience: religious censorship of the arts remains at issue. Comfortably ensconced in Berlin, where he has lived for over a decade, he continues to make art. A recent installation, *White Flag*, consists of American flags that have been covered in a pale glaze. An officer of the Order of Canada with an honorary degree, he now attaches the title of "healer" to his biography.

We all hope to experience standing before a work of art when light and clarity come together to give a feeling of timeless peace, a cosmic ring of truth. I had that moment in '91 viewing the baby seals of *Fin de Siècle*. Even now, through the fog of nostalgia, it heals.

Doing/Writing Queer Research at the Margins
MARIA-BELÉN ORDÓÑEZ

I follow the staircase into a narrow corridor of mirrors where women are sitting along a passageway, on a thin bench against a wall. Despite the darkness, I recognize the angel wing tattoo on one of the woman's bare shoulder blades and sit across from her. Some women are waiting for a massage and I can't help but interrogate their patience, "What are you waiting for?" I ask, intentionally standing away from the lineup. "Erotic Massage but she's taking a long time in there," the woman with the tattooed angel wing replies, her eyes fixed on the "occupied" sign hanging on the closed door. We all laugh and our permissive glances lead us towards each other without a single word. We make a mess of the foggy mirrors, forgetting about the sanctity of privacy. Someone has massage oil and they generously pour the warm silky liquid into our cupped hands. No longer are women obediently waiting for a private erotic massage in this dark corridor of mirrors. Instead, they are playing, laughing and connecting. Traces of our play mark the smooth surface of the mirrors in the tight and increasingly hot corridor as we temporarily discard the prescribed lineup for the unpredictability and optimism of collective desires. Another public moment, I think to myself, where strangers meet and submit their resources and skills to pleasure.

As a queer feminist, doing feminist queer research in Canada, I've been thinking a lot about the significance of passing on knowledge between and among (feminist) generations. For some Western feminists, knowledge that is passed on is about preserving recognized codes of resistance to patriarchy and for some other feminists, it's about reclaiming the messiness of pleasure and resistance because not all paths of resistance are desirable or even possible in all places and times. A quick survey of feminist views on sex work and pornography quickly uncovers, for example, the false assumption that there is an easily identified and universal feminist position on any subject.

What is satisfyingly queer (at least for me) is the capacity to divert from safe and familiar paths and spaces. Western feminist narratives that advocate for equality through promises of inclusion and reversals of power are often not that removed from a patriarchal system that ultimately only benefits some women. I've learned that actively and persistently doubting hegemonic feminist practices sparks interesting and sometimes uncomfortable questions that talk back to power in unexpected ways. Perhaps my queer perversion is in the joyful discovery of productive contradictions for thinking, feeling and becoming queer in the first place. "What are we waiting for?"

The idea that feminists should think and act a certain way by supporting claims of sisterhood while denouncing the appearance of contradictory feminist practices has never felt queer, even when the declared goals are to build better worlds. Obedience leaves a bad taste in my mouth and so disobedience inevitably lives in my research—lives in those opportune locations of play and observation. It's where public culture is made and it's where I've simultaneously been both "at home" and completely undone.

My research has dealt with the sensory experiences, sensations and agents of Canadian media headlines; with narratives of desire and the charged milieus of dance floors and steamy corridors in Toronto women and trans bathhouses; in packed courtrooms where gay young male strippers defended their right to work and strip for older gay men; and in the production of images and texts that addressed child/adult relations while in conversation with the now deceased and well-known, self-declared Canadian advocate of intergenerational love and transgressive writing, John Robin Sharpe. These and other contested sites of pleasure, dialogue and performance were also sites of self-realization and of undoing; of active refusal and critique, and of queer affirmations not easily passed on in the name of resistance. Some of these moments are what cultural critic Jack Halberstam describes as "counter-intuitive" feminism because resistance is negotiated in ways that are oppositional, yet, not always recognized as such. For example, what kind of affinity could a feminist have with a boy-loving older gay man whose transgressive writing featured the agency of young boys in a man's world?

The initial reluctance with which I approached John Robin Sharpe's love of boys moved me towards his literary work not as an advocate of child pornography but as a sensing body affected by the provocations of unknown and unspeakable desires. The necessity to connect with Sharpe's embodied knowledge was mediated by revisiting the work of Montreal-based visual artist Dominique Pepin, whose stunning photographic images of children and adults in natural landscapes highlighted their sensuality in response to Canada's obscenity laws (in the early 90s). Between her images and Sharpe's stories I came to appreciate the difficulty of writing and reading in the space of intergenerational desire where the power dynamics of age, class and gender couldn't be ignored but still needed something other than a simple analysis that turned young people into victims of adults. My affinities are with public intimacies that are propelled by those who live and work on the margins. For me, this is what speaks to a queer feminist ethic of care that isn't fearful of difference. It's the same fearlessness that inspires social change and that talks back to power through planned and spontaneous public events, organized and unorganized exhibitions, movements of all kinds, writing and activism.

There is no doubt that my research about and alongside pleasure-seeking queers in Canada is where I've encountered my own assumptions about the politics of queer desire. John Robin Sharpe's photographic collection of young boys and the legal challenges that this ensued necessarily ruptured my image of the pedophile. His initial acquittal in the late 90s inspired a number of panic reactions, some of which had a renewed concern to "protect children" in the place of protecting freedom of expression. The result was the zealous efforts of police to track the youth in Sharpe's photographs more than 20 years after they had been taken. In 2002 they found one of the youths from his photographs and Sharpe was arrested again and charged with gross indecency. He was found guilty of "indecent assault" and sentenced to two years in prison in 2004. This conviction was not a result of a guilty admission, since Sharpe contended that the relationship he developed with the youth was consensual. Likewise, and in a twist of courtroom revelations, the plaintiff at the *voir dire* in February 2004 also admitted to no harm by Sharpe and highlighted instead his fondness for an older man who cared for him. I came to understand that intergenerational relationships are not inherently exploitative; however, their scrutiny and stigma, like other social stigmas, can inspire a cultural rejection from those who must contend with judgement about their relationship choices.

I joined Sharpe during his *voir dire* in Vancouver and I was interested in the stories that Sharpe recounted, some of which were in connection to the charges, while other stories reflected the reality of living at the margins of desire. It was nonetheless the interconnections, encounters, and intensities in Sharpe's life that reflected an ethics of care for, and in the name of, the Other. The risk is in the capacity to affect and be affected and I found it necessary to connect with Sharpe through the narratives he wrote, and the stories he shared with me, of loving boys.

Time spent with Sharpe included audio recordings of an eclectic array of conversations with him in Vancouver, spanning eight days, three of which were spent in court during Sharpe's *voir dire*. Sharpe's literary work became central to our discussions about boy-love. Between his writing and the reality of his legal proceedings, the tracking of desire and pleasure-seeking nurtured a palpable tension in what was to be part of my research about queer pleasures. Sharpe had an unpredictable impact that did not keep me at a safe distance. I was emotionally and intellectually invested in tracking narratives of justice and desire without trying to fit into Sharpe's world. His tales of boy-love were not stories that held my own desire captive, per se. They were, however, narratives that moved Sharpe and in doing so, moved me as well. Reaching towards these unknowable desires meant foregoing safe landings or familiar feelings.

Beyond the court's interest in visual evidence, photographs of young people already invoke a tableau that places the photographer's proximity to his/her subject/object close and sometimes too close for the moral comfort of some or for the perceived circle of innocence that is supposed to naturally surround all children. Sharpe's interest in snapping pictures of young men was not removed from his general interest in taking pictures or his ethnographic-styled writing, which often described the regard he had for the youth that he met.

For Sharpe, the camera served as a recorder of affective connections. I soon discovered the immediacy and intensity that flowed between his photographs, his writing and the descriptions of the intimate relationships that ensued. A cynical interpretation of his photographic collection might negate the moment of regard, and relegate the images to trophies. Still, what is interesting about Sharpe's photographs is that the photographed subjects also obtained and determined the fate of the photographs. In some cases, they demanded not only to be photographed (for personal use) but they seemed to have directed and composed their interactions with Sharpe and with whomever they were with. In other words, they performed for the camera as bodies with agency and not as objects of a male gaze. It wasn't enough to try and interpret the motivations behind Sharpe's photographs, provided we look by refusing to look habitually, or with persistent clichés. The exchange therefore cannot be reduced to a dominant male gaze that swallows whole the essence of childhood and that gives nothing in return.

Sharpe's stories were intrinsically tied to a complex exchange that was intergenerational and expressed in a format that included visually rendering his experiences. It is the face-to-face encounter that complicates a surfaced domination and alternatively demands something from the person who supposedly has more power. Sharpe was confronted with an obligation to engage, similar to my own obligation as a researcher to listen to him. There are elements in these exchanges that make up moments in which one feels for the

Other—for differences outside of our own frames in understanding the world.

While I was in Vancouver, Sharpe found an opportunity to show me his travel albums as a way to elaborate on some of his stories or to simply put a face to a name—"That is so and so I told you about" he would say with delightful glee, pointing to a radiant and smiling Filipino boy. Up until that point Sharpe and I had been meeting in bars and restaurants where we were forced to speak louder than usual and I was forced to imagine the expressions and movements of the characters that made up his life and writing. Since Sharpe was slowly losing his hearing, this tended to make us both raise our voices and our conversations in public often piqued the interest of neighbouring tables. Meeting in his living space was a welcomed contrast, although this did not necessarily mean that we talked more, and looking at pictures with him generated long and thoughtful silences. I was captivated by a world that featured more youth than adults.

Sharpe's east-side Vancouver room at the time of my visit was cozy despite the harsh noises outside his door, which we chose to ignore. From the outset, Sharpe looked forward to showing me where he lived as one way to demonstrate his fortitude. Living on the east side of Vancouver is not the safe artist colony, gentrified loft, or inspirational geography sought out by some writers. Listening to the audio recording of this meeting prompted me to pay attention to the background noises against stories of travel in the Philippines. Turning pages with him, with an undecipherable argument-noise in the corridor outside his door, undid much of the previous perceptions I had of Sharpe back in 2000, when the media had created a persona akin to Marquis de Sade.

The maverick image of him back in those days was one of arrogance and literary cachet, supported by artists and academics who defended freedom of expression. Contrarily, the man who shared his photographs with me in 2004 was far from arrogant or privileged. During one of our conversations in a Chinese restaurant, I took note of the fortune cookie that Robin had randomly selected. I remember him reading it out loud, "An uncomfortable situation will soon be eased." At the time I thought of the anguish that the law had caused him and hoped that the court proceedings would improve for my friend-interlocutor, whom I did not deem to be a criminal. Years later I can appreciate the value of this fortune cookie for queer perverts who take risks and find solace in building new and active communities, regardless of their ephemerality.

My time with Canada's political and literary pedophile was not a meeting of differing world-views necessarily, nor was it the clashing of moral approaches that had to be worked out in the process. Sharpe, the child pornographer, lover of boys and lover of tales with boys—used his creativity to connect intensely, relentlessly undoing the predictable body on the margins of erotic literature and travel tales. He blurred the imaginary by making it an extension of the real without warning, preambles, or permission. John Robin Sharpe became an important figure in my research not only because he led me to consider the limitations and blunt instrument of the law, and certainly not because he had an explicit feminist position. He pushed instead an unyielding determination to challenge the law and in doing this he stirred the usual pathways that control the image of the child as always vulnerable. Shannon Bell, feminist philosopher at York University, was also well aware that Sharpe's unyielding force had political significance for perverts at the margins.

I was initially drawn to Sharpe's case while a graduate student at York University and I observed that Professor

Shannon Bell had been an ally of Sharpe's during the initial child pornography charges. I was intrigued with Bell's public defense of Sharpe because she articulated what many feminists could not because "feminists tend to equate sexualized writings and images of persons under eighteen years old—and in more lenient versions under fourteen years old—as child sex abuse" (Bell, 2010:87). It was Shannon Bell who secured my meeting with Sharpe and it was Bell who inspired me to pay attention to different feminist practices of transgression. Bell broke from the idea of "passing on" feminist knowledge that confined itself to reproducing the same and recognizable, and Sharpe's resistance to power wasn't always obvious or safe. According to Shannon Bell, "it was this willingness to go the distance for his beliefs rather than plead guilty that interested me more than Sharpe's writings or images per se. The action of writing highly objectionable literary material and using it to initiate a constitutional challenge to Canada's child pornography law got my attention; it was Sharpe's personal fortitude that held it" (ibid:86).

I travelled to Montreal in January of 2013 to visit Robin Sharpe in the hospital after he had surgery to remove a cancerous tumour from his liver in November of 2012. Once a prolific writer, and rebel of the law, Robin Sharpe no longer had the energy to write or read. The books by his bedside were neatly piled at his reach, but he was no longer interested in reaching out for them. His eyes, he explained, had become tired and he opened them only to speak or make clear his rejection of something. When I had proposed to read from a book of his choice, his refusal was only partially linked to his overall exhaustion. This exhaustion was not only the result of pain, depression, or even the loss of appetite that had, by the time I arrived, resulted in malnourishment. He was intentionally and wilfully shedding the flesh from the importance it once had. In his words, "nothing mattered." Past connections to academics and legal minds fascinated by Sharpe's legal challenges gently moved away, while a small circle of mostly young gay men continued to show their support.

It wasn't long before Sharpe regained his strength and we were once again communicating; however, it was the last time that I saw him. He died on August 27, 2015 in a hospital near Vancouver, BC. His passing moved me to think once more of our exchanges, especially during a time that his public persona began to unravel, and he was no longer in the spotlight. Perhaps it was also during this time that I came to better articulate the kind of queer feminist thinking that mattered to me.

"What are we waiting for?" It's no wonder that my impatience for new feminist practices and public queer intimacies has me thinking about passing on fearless knowledge in spite of ongoing power relations. But the knowledge need not be about preserving recognized codes of feminist resistance. Instead, research that urges me to listen otherwise and to feel with continues to agitate for a queer politics that refuses to ever be entirely known.

Sources

Bell, Shannon. "The Perverse Aesthetic of a Child Pornographer: John Robin Sharpe" in *Fast Feminism* (Autonomedia: 2010).

Halberstam, Jack. "Shadow Feminisms: Queer Negativity and Radical Passivity" in *The Queer Art of Failure* (Duke University Press: 2011).

Downtown
KARLEEN PENDLETON-JIMÉNEZ

"Sex was the glue.
If I hadn't been desperate for sex, I wouldn't have fuckin' come out."

1974

He sits in the middle of the running track at Riverdale Park, reading a small magazine. He is 23 years old. If anyone comes towards him, he will be able to see the person a quarter mile away. That will be enough time to jump up, stuff the magazine into his bag, and head off. He looks at the pages, but maintains his peripheral vision. The breeze blows on the cool, spring afternoon, the grass slightly damp underneath his jeans. He can't be seen with this magazine.

It is a magazine about gay liberation. About homosexuals. Nobody has spoken to him about homosexuals. Not his mother or father. Not his church. Not his school. Only briefly and vaguely did it arise on his wanderings across Europe and Asia, in a glance from another man at the hostel; he looked away. There was also the invitation to join another man's shower, and that could really only mean one thing, but he wasn't ready. He was desperate to touch another man, but that doesn't mean he could do it. The only homosexuals he'd known for sure were the ones from TV. During his last year of high school, backlit shadowy figures appeared on screen when Trudeau decriminalized homosexuality. It wasn't a crime anymore, but that doesn't mean it could be fully seen, fully visible to upstanding members of the community. It doesn't mean he could be seen with this magazine. He looks up again but nobody is coming.

It wasn't so easy to get his hands on the magazine. He had to find a store that carried it. He had to find a way to buy it without drawing too much attention. Just because you have the money to pay for it, and just because they're selling it, doesn't mean you're not still doing something wrong. Something illicit. But one can be clever about such transactions. There are *Popular Mechanics* and *Maclean's* to shield his small gay magazine. The magazine itself can hide for almost the whole time. It emerges just for a moment, for a glimpse at the price by the cashier before it is deposited into a bag. And if he waits until there are no other customers nearby, then only the cashier would know. And the cashier might not know for sure that *The Body Politic* is a gay magazine, or if he does, he might forget it, or feel confused by the *Popular Mechanics*. Homosexuals wouldn't buy *Popular Mechanics*.

He flips through his magazine. There is an ad for a march. A Gay Pride March. He could do a march. He couldn't do a bar or a bathhouse. He grew up in a dry town, without bars of any kind, and he's not sure what a bathhouse is. He couldn't be that kind of gay man. Those places are too terrifying. But he could be a gay man in a protest. He knew how to pick up a sign, yell slogans, and march with a group of people down the street. He had been a part of many marches and protests. He is an activist. He is a Marxist. Marching is possible.

166

It would be visible though. There could be cameras. He could stand on the sidewalk and watch. It could just be coincidence that he is there at that moment, while the march is going by. There must be others, shoppers, people out for lunch. He could just be one of them. They are public sidewalks, nothing specifically incriminating, nothing that could tie him directly to the march of gay liberators. Or would people guess, anyway, or would he be caught at the edge of a photo in the papers? Just in case, he should have a plan. What could he do if he saw journalists? He could hold his breath. If he held his breath long enough, he would die. Without oxygen, a person would have a heart attack, and just die, wouldn't they?

He might as well just die, jump off a bridge or something, if he doesn't go to the march. The longing for a man's body has become too unbearable. First it was just one man, just one specific man he followed for four years. He loved him, only him. Just needed to be close to that one body. But that never happened, and it not happening did not seem to stop the wanting of that man, or of other men.

1964

"When you're alone and life is making you lonely
You can always go downtown
When you've got worries, all the noise and the hurry
Seems to help, I know, downtown."

—Petula Clark, "Downtown."

Petula kept repeating "downtown, downtown." As a call, "downtown, downtown," pulling at his young teenage body, downtown. But downtown is a dangerous place. He is a Beaverton boy, a good boy, good grades, no trouble in the community, the son of the man who opened the new and prosperous lumber store. The two annual treks to Toronto for the Eatons display and the Exhibition are exhilarating, but never enough, never enough time. He lags behind his parents and they have to call out to keep him moving.

His father came from "country folk," from farmers, not business owners. His father had been a worker, a repairman at a bicycle store who managed to get a job at a lumber store and then save the money to open his own. But he didn't forget where he came from, and he paid a decent salary to workers, with health benefits, and Christmas dinners with the family. His mom broke her own boundaries, a woman going to school to be a dental nurse. The boy is not aware of the nuances of his family's social climb, but he does know that he is treated well.

If a new kid came to town, he knows to ask two questions: What's your name and what church do you go to? His family are the descendants of Irish and Scottish immigrants, but always Orange. His family is Presbyterian. They are not as affluent as the Anglicans, not as progressive as the United Church, but good, solid Protestants nonetheless. His mother teaches him from the bible how Martin Luther King from the television will free the "slaves" just as Moses had. There are also Catholics in their town of a thousand, but he doesn't know them. They don't go to his school anymore. They are kept somewhere else.

He is fascinated by somewhere else. His father comes home from a lumberman's convention with a handful of foreign money. Different smells, different images, different languages. He likes holding the colourful paper in his hands, pieces of the world. It means those places are real. It means people live there and use the different money and he would like to meet them. He hunts through the encyclopedia, matching the curves of letters, the structures of symbols, to their national origins.

Beaverton is built upon the mouth of Lake Simcoe, the force of the Beaver River powering a mill and attracting a community. From this vantage point, the waterways lead up and around the towns and farmlands of Ontario, and across two great lakes. The sky reflects on the water and opens a vast, blue-grey space. A distance farther than he can see.

At 18, he will flee his tiny village and be the first one in his family to go to university, but that won't hold him. It won't be far enough away. He is a young white man, after all, and his school books told the history of white men exploring the world, so why shouldn't he? The cold war has frozen the battles, and he is free to wander. He will drop out of school and escape, travelling across North Africa, Yugoslavia, Tunisia, Turkey, Iran, Afghanistan, Pakistan, India, Nepal. Each land, each people, washing over him. Each religion, Buddhists, Hindus, Muslims shedding the hell and brimstone pounded into a childhood by a minister all dressed in black, screaming at him, and his family and community, "If you don't believe…You're going to burn and your skin will come off!!" But, if each place has its own distinct deities, its own fears, its own preachers of right and wrong, if all of these different people feel just as strongly as they had back home, then none of these beliefs are the truth. The solid material truth. The lord's creation, the wide vibrant world, undoes him, releases him from sin.

1981

It's after midnight. There is pounding on his bedroom door. His body is weak from a flu, and exhausted from studying economics schema that mean nothing to him. There are graphs of the price of potatoes dancing through his dreams. The exam is in the morning. Economics 101, one of the big early year courses at the University of Toronto where they like to fail half the students. He doesn't want to fail.

The pounding resumes. "Gerald Hannon's on the phone," one of his housemates yells, "He says it's urgent." Gerald Hannon was another member of *The Body Politic*. It's the same magazine that delivered him to his first PRIDE March, to his first male lover, to his first books about gay liberation. It wasn't long before he joined the magazine himself, taking on the international news. He has been their "bonafide politico," a man who travels across the world, who studies Marxism and racism, who advocates for workers' rights (Bébout).

Gerald's instructions were clear and direct. "They're raiding all the baths. You're closest to the Club. Get over there right away."

He doesn't even go to the baths. It isn't his scene. He's cursing the full 10-minute walk over to the club in the frozen February night with his housemate. He wishes Richard was here and not away. His lover now of 6 years. His companion on adventures. Richard is a fellow Marxist, and a filmmaker. He is Chinese from Trinidad. They have found family in one another, and filled their communal home with friends from all over the world. They have travelled the globe together, and he wishes Richard was here beside him as he walks into this unknown.

The police are everywhere on the street. They are lions smugly devouring their prey. They prey on men. Confused, scared, and defiant men. Nearly 300 men of every ethnicity, race, class. Men whose jobs and marriages might be over now with their newly acquired criminal charges of being found in a common bawdy house. The men are in the open on the dark night. The bathhouse has spilled onto the street for everyone to see. That's not the way it's supposed to happen. The bathhouses have been there for decades. They are an open secret. The gays can do what they want if they are discreet, contained, hidden encounters late into the night. The police have broken the rules, and brought their bodies out for all the public to see.

He sees them. He sees their bodies, their baffled faces, regular men interrupted in an everyday activity. They are not scandalous, not scary. They are men he might know, or want to know. He approaches the men who go to bathhouses, and asks what happened. He transforms into gay journalist and activist, documenting their stories. They have their own questions. There is a Portuguese man, a construction worker. "They arrested me. They say I have to go to court." They asked for employers' names. They asked for their wives' names. Will their names be published in the paper? Will everyone know? He doesn't know the answer.

He doesn't do very well on his test in the morning. He shakes it off and races on his bicycle over to the office of *The Body Politic*. It is the biggest gay organization in town, the one with an office, a concrete piece of the city that belongs to gays. And it is bustling with activists planning a protest. When, he wonders? Tonight. Tonight they will have a protest. They will protest along Yonge Street. But that's not possible. It's not safe to protest at night, and certainly not on Yonge Street. Yonge Street is Toronto's artery. It's sacred, the one uninterrupted path designed by city founders as an escape from American invaders. It's filled with heterosexual bars, drunk men who could spill out and beat them. Nobody blocks Yonge Street. It's too soon besides. Protests involve planning. There are marshals to be assigned, maps to be printed, permits to be obtained, do we even have a phone tree?

"We don't need a fuckin' permit," a tough looking dyke cuts him off. She gathers up the flyers and heads out. He shakes his head. He is afraid. He has organized revolutionaries and it's hard to get people out on the street.

He will go and support gay liberation and hope they are not beaten.

When he arrives around 9 o'clock there are already 40 to 50 people on the street. All right, that's a positive sign; it's not so easy for police or drunks to beat up 40 to 50 people marching together. We might be ok. The crowd keeps growing. Where are they coming from? There are runners out at every gay bar, every bath, spreading the word. The people fill across the width of Yonge Street and down. Who are they? Three hundred and nine men were arrested last night. Are they here? If it's not them, it's their friends. Three hundred and nine people and their friends and gay liberationists are a lot of people. By midnight there are 2000. They have shut down Yonge Street. They are no longer willing to tolerate the whims of the police.

The police are furious. The police are surprised. Why are these homosexuals so upset? Who knew they had so many friends? They are only doing their job. They are only maintaining the morality of their beloved city.

He already knows about police harassment. They raided *The Body Politic* office four years ago. They scared them, shuffling off with their boxes, supplies, mailing lists, all of the addresses of all of their subscribers. Still not returned. It had been terrifying, all those vulnerable names in the hands of the police. And yet, nothing has really happened. The police scared them, but *The Body Politic* won in court. Therefore police raids and charges might not mean so much. The uniforms and official business and stomping around was a big display. A threatening performance. He had been sitting in the office working when they came. He had survived. *The Body Politic* had survived. There had been court costs, time, aggravation, publicity. They were activists trying to promote gay liberation, trying to be noticed, and the court and trial in part offered a forum.

When they ask him to speak, he is an activist, and he is not afraid. He can see the situation with clarity. The outcome is logical. Past raids have yielded no convictions. The police, therefore, have no reason to attack, other than to invoke fear. He can explain the operation and function of the raids. He becomes a spokesperson for the newly formed The Right to Privacy Committee, and simply explains to the papers how the raids are "so ridiculous. I think the public is going to recognize that what we're facing isn't simply criminal charges, but in fact a vendetta" ("Police mounting vendetta, homosexual spokesmen say").

It could be a vendetta against *The Body Politic* for successfully beating the police in court, or politicians publically supporting gay people. It could be a vendetta against gays shamelessly coming out of the closet, declaring their rights en masse. Somebody needs to put them back in their place.

But a vendetta is so dramatic. So irrational. Police are supposed to be reasoned protectors of the public, not driven by vendettas to stomp around the community. He is supposed to be the homosexual, the freak. He is not a freak. He is the clear-headed one in the newspaper, and the police are the ridiculous ones. He is the man appealing to the intelligence and good sense of the public to see this.

They see it. They see him. Everyone across the nation sees him. Beaverton sees him. His father sees him. It's one thing to know your son is gay, and quite another for your entire town to know it as well.

There is screaming in Beaverton in their big rambling house. The son and father fight it out. The mother cries.

The Presbyterian silence is shattered. He is ready for this. He has seven years of gay activism under his belt. He has become strong.

1992

The gay community is dying around him. He might die too.

When Michael Lynch asked him 6 years ago to join AIDS Action Now!, he didn't really know how he might contribute. How does one go about protesting a disease? What good are marches and speeches against microscopic invaders? He didn't know anything about medicine. But off he went to the meeting, because they asked him. He often doesn't choose his causes, they choose him. He is a good talker. He knows how to explain things in a way that everyone understands. He offers examples that tie an issue to an object, to a memory, to some material experience in your life. His tone is sensible and intelligent. You believe him because you want to be sensible and intelligent too. He is also nice to look at. He is not very fashionable for a gay man in his t-shirts and chinos but he is tall, handsome, and fit. He has bright blue eyes and a trim brown beard. He is ready for the cameras. He sparkles and the community needs everyone now, especially its stars.

He cannot argue with a virus, but he can advocate for better treatment of hospital patients. He cannot find a cure, but he can demand money for research. It began with Pentamidine. If you place the drug in an aerosol inhaler instead of an IV, you could save a person's life. You could prevent or kill the pneumonia. The Canadian government wanted tests to prove it. They didn't trust the American lives already being saved. There are proper procedures. There are professional methods for approval. There will be placebos.

It is a devastating math problem. It is a 6-month test of 300 people. 150 patients take Pentamidine, 150 are given placebos. 18 percent of the participants taking the placebo will probably contract pneumonia. 18% of 150 = 27. Of those, up to half could die, 13. 13 people would die because the Canadian government would not trust Americans surviving PCP pneumonia.

He was there to fight for those 13. He was there to fight using his words and his clever comparisons. He was there at the protest where coffins for the future dead were carried up the steps of the hospital. He told the *Globe and Mail*, "If you were talking about an acne cream, I could understand waiting to see who got the most pimples…But placebo trials are totally inappropriate for people who are suffering from a life-threatening illness" (Toughill). The government is inappropriate. They are concerned about pimples and he is there to discuss a human life. In one metaphor, he elevates the worth of gay men's lives, and simultaneously diminishes the expert knowledge of government medicine.

He facilitates meetings through Paulo Freire's popular education techniques, building literacy based on the experiences of the audience. He has learned that their collective knowledge might just be more useful than the doctor's readings of the latest reports. The doctors are at least as blind as them. This is uncharted territory. It is not an intellectual exercise. The ability of activists to gather stories, information, to chart lives and deaths, to observe, to critique, and demand will save lives.

There are beepers going off. Every few minutes. Alerts tied to the bodies of the men around him in the meeting. Beepers that measure time. Beepers that call for another dose of AZT. The beepers put him on edge. The ring is jarring. He watches pale, weak bodies twitch at the sound, consume the medication in a timely fashion, and become weaker still.

It's reached that point. He has held out as long as possible, not wanting to consume the toxic drugs on top of the damage from the virus. The number is bad. 50 T cells, the doctor tells him, when it's supposed to be at 1000. He will have to start taking the medicines. He has watched carefully. He has informed himself. He directs the doctor on his prescription, a balance of medications, a low dose of AZT. This is his best shot, he decides. The doctor argues, if there are only 3 medications, and he runs through two, and their potency fades...if his time runs out? It's too big of a risk. It's not the recommended procedure. He demands the risk. He is weighing every meeting, every newspaper article, every medical report, every friend and lover who has died. He hopes time won't run out.

Richard loves him. Richard will stay with him. Sickness doesn't scare Richard. Richard grew up with a very sick sister. Richard knows all about dying. The world might want to quarantine him until he disappears, but not Richard. Richard loves him.

Epilogue: 2000 (plus)

"You two should meet each other," Didi Khayatt, my professor at York University maneuvers us together, "This is Tim McCaskell." A tall man in his forties with salt and pepper hair holds out his hand to me. He smiles and asks me about my work. He looks me right in the eye. I am a twenty-eight-year-old Chicana dyke from California, recently relocated to Toronto. We are attending a social justice education conference. He works for the Toronto District School Board Equity Department. By the year end he helped me to publish my first book *Are You a Boy or a Girl?*, and distribute it across the region.

When I met Tim my mother had been dead for less than 5 years. She had died suddenly of pneumonia at 55, and I was there rubbing her hand when the life disappeared from her. I remember thinking as I saw her body lying still on the hospital gurney that I could die at any time. My mom had not expected to die that day. She hadn't had the chance to say goodbye to anyone and her kitchen still had bags of flour and chocolate chips out on the counter for holiday fudge-making. I felt so sad for my mom losing her life quickly and easily. I felt devastated that my main protector was gone. I also felt incredible bravery, because I might die quickly too and so I might as well live exactly as I wished.

I wished to always be an out dyke, fighting against homophobia, with a lover who was equally unashamed. I wished to fight against racism, which had hurt my Chicana/o communities and every person of colour I knew. I wished to become a writer and educator who could work on creating beauty in words to challenge hatred. Despite my convictions, I still found the daily acts of activism wearing me down. I remember a meeting where I was trying to convince a group of white gay committee members to include at least some content by queers of colour into the program but they refused. I remember trying to hold it together in front of them so they wouldn't see the tears that fell out of me. I remember the pain in my stomach of not being able to call my mother for advice later that night. I remember how small I felt. It's hard to maintain bravery when you can't call your mother anymore.

Meeting Tim helped me tremendously on two fronts. He is not a parent but he is a mentor, someone who is older and more experienced with education and activism. I can find his insights in his writing, speeches, and Facebook, and sometimes when I'm really lucky he drives all the way to Peterborough, Ontario to work with my students and I. His solid presence, the vitality of his queer body, the insistence of his political philosophy, all comfort me. Even when I don't see him for a while, I know that he is there and I find myself citing his ideas to my students. Sometimes I find him in my daydreams when I second-guess myself. I feel stronger, more courageous, and more entitled to fight. He's with me when I go into schools and do workshops with children and youth surviving homophobia. He's with me when I have the patience to listen and educate university students who think sexism doesn't exist. He's with me when I gracefully convince my bosses to adopt some new social justice activity. He's not the only person who guides me, but he is an important one. I don't know why it works that way. Why a man who lives a couple miles away from me, from a different land, a different ethnicity, a different generation, a different sex, could so profoundly affect me. I just know how brave he helps me feel. That's probably why, in the mountain of information about his life, I was drawn to write about the terrifying moments when he chose bravery as a way forward.

Tim has become a producer of social justice phenomena: conferences, workshops, political organizing. He is the man you call if it's imperative that a certain audience understand the way racism or sexism or classism or homophobia operate. He can get gay organizations to care about racism, and male-dominated workplaces to listen to women. He makes things happen. He doesn't give participants definitions, he creates experiences that are unforgettable. You can watch him online at his best, "Neoliberalism as a Water Balloon" (Eigenberger).

A silver-haired man with clear blue eyes looks right at me through the computer screen. He wears a lab coat and a straight face. Nothing in particular is humorous about the subject matter of neoliberalism, nor with the careful articulation of stratified power and money based on social groupings. And yet, his very seriousness is comical. He shows the destructive consequences through a bursting water balloon, performing as if he's a science teacher.

Tim was my entry into a Toronto culture, a group of activists of different races, classes, genders, sexualities 20 years older than me, who have dedicated their lives to social change for everyone. The community is far from utopic and Tim is not perfect, but the experience is hopeful and unusual. I'm not saying there aren't white guys in California who care deeply about racism, I'm just saying I haven't met any of them. And I wonder what strange world I have come upon. And I want to know what made this man.

I am forever an activist in need of ideas and language. I am forever a butch in need of masculine role models. I am forever a queer in need of love for my body and desire.

I think of Tim today, still speaking, still organizing, still loving Richard, still visiting bathhouses. I think of him in a bathhouse relishing the fun. Many worlds collide in this sacred gay space: friendships are made, community connections solid-ified, some men come out, some go home ashamed. Tim is part of the hungering for men's bodies, bodies of all colours, builds, smells. He searches for them at the end of a workday: CEOs, mechanics, accountants, filmmakers, janitors. He puts faith in their pleasure together and one more story shared.

Notes

The majority of the information in this chapter is taken from an interview I conducted with Tim McCaskell at his home in Toronto on March 25th, 2015. The narrative is shaped by my interpretation of his words.

Chicana/os are people of Mexican descent living in the United States, often with left-leaning political convictions. The term became popularized through The Chicano Movement, a civil rights movement in the 1960s and '70s.

Sources

Bébout, Rick. "Baby Steps: Late 1971 through 1974," Jan. 2000. Web. Mar. 2015. http://www.rbebout.com/oldbeep/baby.htm

Eigenberger, Martin. "Neoliberalism as a Water Balloon," Oct. 2011. Web. Apr. 2015. https://www.youtube.com/watch?v=XIUWZnnHz2g

"Petula Clark Lyrics: Downtown," AZLyrics.com. 2000–2015. Web. Apr. 2015. http://www.azlyrics.com/lyrics/petulaclark/downtown.html

"Police mounting vendetta, homosexual spokesmen say." *The Globe and Mail* (1936—Current); Apr 24, 1981; ProQuest Historical Newspapers: The Globe and Mail.

Toughill, Kelley. "AIDS, HIV patients face loss of 'expert' care. Proposed restrictions on new doctors may take toll on city clinic: [SA2 Edition]." *Toronto Star.* May 8, 1993. Torstar Syndication Services, a Division of Toronto Star Newspapers Limited. Mar 25, 2015.

Queer Intimacies of Anarchism
ROBERT TEIXEIRA

*Neither Saint-Simon, nor Karl Marx, nor Marlo, nor Bakun-
in. Instead, the reforms that are best suited to our own bodies.*
—José Martí, 1890

Dedicated to Sam "Tumbleweed" Roberts (1986–2007)

"**A**narchy is Freedom." These words, I soon learned, were
inscribed in bold Yiddish characters on the back of his
leather biker jacket, framed by chains that looped down
from his right shoulder. His ensemble was completed with
skin-tight ripped, faded jeans and super polished 12-hole,
black Doc Martens. To top it off he wore a T-shirt blaring
"AIDS Infected Faggot." Confrontational style.

I was smitten. At the time, I was a twenty-two-year-old
English student at the University of Toronto, wide-eyed and
a little nervous, standing, mostly immobile with drink in
hand, scanning the room and curiously eyeing with excitement and fascination what was a sheer spectacle of difference between him and the other patrons in the bar. I was
captivated by that sight. He was standing alone, no one was
talking to him, it seemed like he was in the centre of a magical circle that admitted no one except the very audacious. It

was 1992 and we were at Woody's, perhaps the most popular gay bar in town.

Looking back, this memory is dominated by a meeting with someone whom I felt shared my feeling of being apart. At the same time we harboured a mild derision for a crowd that was too preppy—a hangover from an '80s teenage sojourn in the gender-bending and freaky post-punk and Goth style and music that was my source of pride (and a portal of escape from the stultifying environs of the Scarborough Catholic high school culture I had had to endure). I recognized that style. My eyes were drawn to him as if Nina Hagen herself was standing there. I was surprised to encounter someone like him here. I will call him Raven. And for a long while my own political mentoring was a form of submersion in his political discourse and like a queer boy that desperately wants to get fucked for the first time, it filled my own thinking and desires.

Emboldened by drink and the press of sex and curiosity, I approached him first. "Hi. I'm wondering what the words on the back of your jacket mean. It looks pretty cool." I was hoping he'd show some approval of my own propensity to dress in black. Perhaps I wasn't aware of the degree to which my youth had the power to attract—and once attracted—to retain interest.

He proudly and a bit too loudly responded, giving me a not unfriendly mini-lecture on the history of anarchism and its social justice aims. "It's in Yiddish and it means 'Anarchy is Freedom.' I am a communist-anarchist, and I believe in self-determination for all." Taking a swig of beer he continued, "we are against the state and capitalism and believe in the right of the oppressed to organize themselves in non-authoritarian and non-hierarchical ways. My anarchist-communist ideology stems from Goldman, Bakunin, Kropotkin and Berkman."

There was a strident and at times stentorian tone to Raven's voice, but never an unfriendly gesture, and his speech was marked by friendly glances and an interest in me that kept me riveted in place wanting to hear more and to bask in what seemed like a welcome mutual attention and interest. Eventually I learned that he was in his late 30s, and had been living with HIV/AIDS for a while. He had moved from out west to settle in Toronto. He instructed me to look at the writings of Emma Goldman and Goldman's lover and lifelong comrade, Alexander Berkman, whose *ABC of Communist Anarchism* he suggested was a good place to start.

I am troubled about this writing, and the narrative culled from memories that are tied to a mess of feelings, emotional turmoil, indecision and confusion, that surfaced while writing. I receive memory-feelings of the words not spoken, and the moments when the klaxon of political rhetoric shattered my sense of reality—a none-too subtle collusion stirring within me as I, at times, fought with indecision and ambivalence at the implications of these words.

This became all too clear several years ago when I entered a Ph.D. program and struggled to fund it, without grants or other government funding nor family support. I come from a working-to-lower-middle-class immigrant Portuguese family and both my parents died before I turned 20. Years later, Raven decided that I was the class enemy, and in a public venue began to excoriate me for being an "ivory tower" academic and for essentially taking time to be in graduate school. This was way off the mark and it was a bit of a shock as none of his network of friends, some of which I knew well, came to my defence. A silent collusion of unacknowledged privilege and shackled conversations. Yet before that happened, I was transfixed.

The friendship that developed between Raven and I was one of those moments of intensity in learning, conversation and adventure, but it was also shot through by vituperative disagreements, distrust and a cultivation over time of a studied respectful distance. Mentorship is not something that queers can or should regard with the usual seriousness and unexamined naturalized hierarchies that passes for ethics in our culture. Yet, it is a testament to Raven's radicalism that I never felt the condescension that flows all too easily from middle-aged gay men towards their younger friends.

Yet there were other, less-salubrious, moments. Raven was fond of discussing the nineteenth-century queer intergenerational relationship between the young social revolutionary Sergei Nechaev and the great Russian anarchist, Mikhail Bakunin. I saw similarities between the relationship between Nechaev and Bakunin and the mentorships I was forming with radical gay men almost twice my age. The intimacies of storytelling used by those living for social change I believed created a queer radical conspiracy of hope.

Bakunin took to the young Nechaev with a passion that was immediately recognizable as homoerotic. Raven directed me to an early piece by Charley Shively in Boston's gay liberation paper, *Fag Rag*, a counterpart to Toronto's own *The Body Politic*, that discussed their queer radical bond in the 1870s. Nechaev is the author of the 1869 essay "Catechism of a Revolutionary," and although Raven talked about it in glowing terms, I feigned approval when in fact I felt horror about an essay that subsumed all human feeling and relations to the urgent overthrow of the Tsar. Dostoevsky countered this nihilism in his novel *Demons*, with a character based on Nechaev, as did Joseph Conrad in *The Secret Agent*. These texts functioned as relays for the stereotyped image of the masked and violent bomb-throwing anarchist, a seductive phantasmagoria that, like zombies in our own time, refuses to die.

It was here that a darkening note developed in our friendship foreshadowing the parting in our ideological ways. I encourage everyone to read the essay, it is a sickening example of placing the ends of violent insurrection before all human relationships, love, comradeship or mutuality. It speaks to me as radically counter to the spirit of social justice. For all this, there was also incisive humour, such as the time when Raven, enthusiastic about an ardent young anarchist he had met in Montréal, quipped, "This guy would make Nechaev seem like Margaret Thatcher!"

Back at my place, I was renting the main floor of an old 'war home' in an east-end working-class district, we continued to drink, we smoked a joint and a mess of beer bottles began to appear. I dropped ecstasy for the very first time, while the recently released CD *Fook* by Pigface played at high volume. It was a memorable evening.

Conversation flowed to sexual practices, feelings, desires, to urgent declarations of struggles to come, and was mixed with a vulnerability cultured in regret over perceived inadequacy in action, courage or commitment. There are times, too infrequent it seems, when two people can experience a kind of heart-mind revelation that in an instant crystallizes a sense of the immense social forces that structure our lives. For a moment there is a clarity of how we've come to be where we find ourselves. It shows our alienation for what it is and how the necessary acts we use day to day that propel us through a capitalist landscape wear out, how they fall away, and how another truth is revealed that is not comforting, nor hopeful. At times like this we gain a sense of the real stakes involved and at the same time sense the unique moment of a bond forged through erotic closeness, a vulnerability of the flesh, and the fragile self we present to the other. This was one of those moments, felt only a handful of times, but which impressed itself deep in my psyche.

Soon after, and spurred by this new friendship, I eagerly sought out titles on anarchism, at Seekers Books. Located in the Annex, a middle-class student enclave in Toronto, I found Rudolf Rocker's *Anarcho-Syndicalism* (Pluto Press, 1989). The book was my first encounter with anarchist thought. I read it in two solid sittings, most of them spent at various cafés between my English literature classes. I wasn't sure what 'syndicalism' meant at the time and thought perhaps that this may have been a poor introduction to the topic. I chose it mostly because it was the only readily identifiable book on the topic I could find on the shelf of this basement used bookstore, popular with students, lefties, and an assortment of others, some down on their luck, new-agers, mystics and the occasional latter-day Sufi in white flowing robes.

Like many other self-identified anarchists I later encountered, I became a bookish radical. Soon my shelves at home filled up with a mess of incendiary titles. A centrepiece of my collection is Peter Marshall's massive tome, *Demanding the Impossible*, an updating of *Anarchism*, by Canada's anarchist "man of letters," George Woodcock. One of the better introductions I discovered was French labour activist and queer anarchist Daniel Guérin's 1970 syndicalist take on anarchism, *Anarchism: From Theory to Practice* introduced by Noam Chomsky. Guérin's writing is now receiving greater attention from English readers in translation. His observations on the rise of the Nazis and their impact on everyday workers in Germany titled *The Brown Plague: Travels in Late Weimar and Early Nazi Germany* should be more widely read.

The nineteenth century loomed large in my conversations with Raven especially the 'classical' anarchist tradition, largely forgotten but whose influence and ideas are re-emerging in critical historical scholarship. It was a revelation for me to make it through Emma Goldman's two-volume auto-biography, *Living My Life*, first published in 1931. A touchstone for queer anarchists: she was an early feminist, a labour radical and advocate for free love who had passionate friendships with other women. Legend has it that in 1892 Goldman raised money through sex work in order to purchase the gun that her comrade and lover, Alexander Berkman, used to wound the anti-worker and union-busting industrialist Frick in a botched *attentat*, a politically motivated assassination with the aim to rouse the working-classes to revolutionary action. It didn't work of course. And while Goldman later revised her ideas on political violence, she took great risks defending comrades who spoke for violence in her public speaking engagements.

Emma Goldman also lived in Toronto in the 1920s and '30s. Decades later, an intrepid group of young queer activists, artists, and hardcore kids, including Toronto artist and founder of the wild queer rock night Vazaleen, Will Munro (1975–2010), opened an anarchist info-shop, named Who's Emma, in the Kensington Market area, an area long established as an immigrant enclave. Last year a Heritage Plaque commemorating Goldman's residency in Toronto was erected near one of the apartments she lived in on Spadina Avenue in Chinatown.

The excitement of my reading led to action on the streets. As a young undergraduate my political knowledge became radicalized both inside and outside the classroom where I attended many community demos and meetings. I learned from mostly queer, trans and socialist-feminist women involved in the women's and queer rights, reproductive justice, sex worker, anti-racist and sex-positive social justice movements. I listened intently and learned much from the passionate orators and urgent declarations amidst angry crowds, to always make connections. The streets, the demos, the meetings, were an education apart from the university education I was struggling to finance.

I was one of only several hundred in front of the U.S. Consulate in 1991 attending a demo organized by the International Socialists protesting the first U.S. invasion of Iraq by George Bush, senior. I was there, in May, 1992, attending protests in Toronto alongside many men and women when Morgentaler's abortion clinic on Harbord Street was fire-bombed. I also attended sombre candlelit marches when in 1989, 14 women in the Engineering program (all around my age) were massacred by a well-armed misogynist at the École Polytechnique in Montréal. I stood shoulder to shoulder with many others against the rise of a reorganized Nazi and anti-immigrant movement in Toronto, and participated with Anti-Racist Action (ARA) in high-risk demos and confrontations with local Nazi boneheads including the infamous Holocaust denying Nazi propagandist, Ernst Zundel whose home on Carlton street we picketed. Zundel was later deported to Germany where he was eventually imprisoned.

These scattered actions eventually came together in the street demos organized by the Toronto Coalition Against Racism (TCAR). Those involved in these social justice movements always strove to make connections. It was where I learned that the fight for reproductive justice is a fight for sexual, social and bodily autonomy. We needed to overcome the interlocking systems of class, racial, sexual inequality that perpetuate and organize oppression and domination.

Raven was a stalwart and a constant presence at these and many more street demonstrations.

I've been politically active to varying degrees and in some form or other for over 20 years. And I have, for better or for worse, become less and less tolerant, and have less energy for dealing with activist "bad manners" and unreflective individuals. This is both a self-preserving realization that sharpened my sense of what is important and where to place my energies, but also it has the tendency to produce new forms of isolation, shame, resentment and general bad feelings.

As I cut my teeth on the theoretical and practical aspects of radical social change, more questions emerged, pushing through the mix of anger, grief and sadness that bespoke the complex catastrophe that enfolds our lives. Paradoxically, the issue of class is a haunting presence on the left. There are many discussions that never happen and are not 'owned' but rather silently elided or disavowed. Activists from solid middle-class backgrounds never understand how their privilege enables their practices, and their disavowal of this contributes to a sense of doubt, confusion and unreality. These are troublesome emotions and a disorienting environment for those of us who are not so well positioned.

Other questions press on me, as when Raven propounded the notion of committing 'class suicide' as a way to gain a kind of activist credibility. "To the barricades!" This type of muscular activist mentality is not too hard to find. If you haven't been in jail, some will pronounce that you are not really committed. Every activist must ask what is 'direct action'? What does 'commitment' mean? How do you know when you or someone else is not 'committed'? What is our understanding of 'commitment'? What does it mean and why are we concerned with how 'committed' we or others are? What does it mean to be uncommitted?

The eye of shame focuses upon the lack of opportunity, the structured limitations and blocks on the transmission of vital knowledge, especially when you're queer and an activist. How do you organize and manage a crowd of hundreds? The fucking cops scare me. How many times have I heard activists say with pride that they were arrested and did time in jail? Hearing this I shrink; the thought makes my stomach churn. Who would bail me out? Most people I know are poor or just managing. And I shudder to think that if thrown in jail I may be one of the forgotten ones.

These unexamined ways of being produce a tendency to moral denunciation and shaming, a mind-bending effluvium that functions as a kind of emotional and intellectual purgative. A lack of self-reflexive awareness, even in the ideas we hold and the analyses we undertake and the forms of actions we are willing to endorse and engage ourselves in, needs to be addressed. What are you doing? What have you done? Scrutinizing ourselves and others—weighing and comparing; have I done enough? Am I enough?

In November the temperature in Leeds, UK can make your teeth chatter uncontrollably even for those used to Canadian winters. The way that damp cold gets into you wasn't something I had anticipated nor prepared for. It was 2006 and I was in Leeds to deliver a paper and participate in a conference that was perhaps the first of its kind, bringing together activists and scholars on the topic of anarchism and sexualities. Leeds was one of the centres of British industry, a centre of worker radicalism in the past, but in recent years its city centre had been largely made over by the outlets of globalized consumerism populated by university students.

During the morning check-in I noticed a young guy who had slipped in with some friends almost as though they were attempting to evade detection. He was tall and lean with longish wild hair and a sweet face. I learned his name was Sam and a tone of openness and sharing was set when he exclaimed during our introductions, "This is the first queer gathering where I didn't feel like I had to get high to be at." And with delicate movements of his thin hands he wiped his long hair away from his eyes as he went on telling all gathered that he was staying with friends in a nearby squat and was nervous to be at a gathering with academics. I was drawn to his honesty and felt the pull of desire, yet I felt he could shun me for representing the 'boring' older academic.

I felt that magnetic pull of someone I would have loved to meet but was nervous at the same time. But I would catch compelling glimpses of him, always surrounded by a gaggle of friends, as we travelled between workshops.

In the afternoon I was scheduled to give my talk. The room was full to capacity. I was giving a paper on the possibilities of child and youth erotic autonomy using queer and post-modern anarchist theories. I knew that giving a paper on childhood and sexuality generates buzz. I was preparing to deliver my paper when Sam strode into the room, alone, and headed to the back. He was wearing a bright yellow oversized T-shirt that read, "Children Be Gay," created by Canadian artist Daryl Vocat. I caught Sam's eye and I followed his path to the back of the room, before I realized that the audience was looking at me. During my introduction I mentioned to him how much I liked his T-shirt and that the artist was from Toronto.

After the conference the participants re-grouped at The Common Ground, a local Social Centre in Leeds, to share a communal vegetarian meal. Sharing meals with others has a long history in organizing on the left as a way to meet immediate needs, and to come together in a convivial way to build trust and friendships. With dinner out of the way, plates started to disappear from the table and folks wandered around, then Sam came by to chat with me. I was glad he had made the first move. I don't think I could hide my enthusiasm. I finally popped the question, "Would you like to come back to my hotel room and hang out, talk, and spend the night together? My hotel isn't far from here."

Sam's eyes lit up, "Yeah, for sure! I'd really like that. Just let me tell my friends that I'm spending the night with you and where I'm going to be." Back at the hotel room we spent a lot of time chatting and in various states of undress we continued to hold each other and make out but mostly we entered an intimate mind-space.

Sam and I reflected on how activist spaces can be oppressive and alienating and how sometimes that keeps me away from some action or collective organizing. I think this is, in part, because we think that fighting the power that we imagine to be completely external to ourselves makes us unable to confront how we treat each other. We imagine that the subtle interpersonal processes involved in how we organize, listen and treat each other are less important than our unmitigated confrontation with the 'system.'

Continuing, we felt that the conference was able to create a more open space for queers and gender nonconforming folks. We both felt, however, for complex social, and experiential reasons, that spaces that tend to be comprised of people of feminist/trans and/or queer experience (people who can never take for granted that our modes of being, our bodies, our loves and desires will find enduring social support) are more aware of the subtle, interpersonal dynamics of power and thus more responsive to taking care of each other. I have experienced these forms of sustenance and find them to be crucially important to the maintenance of long-term adherence to social movements and activist communities. But it is, sadly, not always the case. There are no predetermined guarantees about the nature of any social space. Perhaps that is what makes them so interesting, dangerous and yet filled with possibilities…there are no 'safe' spaces.

I shared with Sam how I arrived to meetings and events with a lesser or greater trepidation each and every time especially in activist and academic contexts. Spaces that are and continue to be dominated by straight white middle-class men, I experienced as less introspective and more apt to be alienating and discomfiting. I am sorry if this is difficult knowledge for some to hear but I count it is as one of the truths that have been produced by a social system as it constructs dominant identities coupled with heaps of disincentives to people to engage in what queer educational theorist Deborah P. Britzman has called the "difficult knowledge" of personal and socio-political introspection and honest self-reflection.

Sam and I discussed how the avenues for healing ourselves were slight. Many are drawn to activism from spaces of hurt, pain, trauma, and the realization of subordination and domination in their own lives. A lack of space and resources for discussion, healing, and transforming difficult emotions, and finding the support we need is important in our work as activists. Many questions came forward while we were holding one another in that small hotel room.

How do we find rest and time for reflection and time away? Do we feel guilty for needing to step back? How do we take care of ourselves and prevent burnout?

"These questions are super important," I responded, as I pulled him closer and stroked the soft skin on the back of his neck and shoulders. I added, "I'm glad we're talking about this. It's important to talk about things like how do we re-energize ourselves and deal with difficult emotions? How do we avoid becoming bitter or cynical? What rejuvenates our desire to work with others for social change?"

We spoke about our histories of activism. I revealed the shame I experienced for not being the one carrying the megaphone or being able to organize a demo. Sam was surprised, and turning to him I smiled and said that I was also incredibly nervous giving my talk today. Sam retorted excitedly, "I had no idea Rob! You looked like you were completely confident up there."

He made connections with the tendency I have to be surprised when people remember me, to my feelings of being invisible or not being taken into account when I was a kid. Due to poor interactional patterns in my working-class upbringing, and being the youngest of three boys, I was often shunted aside and was made to carry the burden of overweening aggression from my older brothers. These are feelings that have dogged me and have contributed, I think, to a sense of inadequacy or not being taken seriously as an adult. This in turn feeds my insecurities around performing as an academic.

How do activists acquire the skills and confidence they need to become 'activists' in ways that are recognized by others? How are activist skills acquired and passed down to others? Which qualities are considered crucial and important, which qualities are deemed less important or unremarkable? How does being queer or gender nonconforming fit into this? How do our working-class histories shape our experiences even within social movements and among our more radical friends and comrades? How do activists become recognized as such and how are their public profiles established? Why are some activists recognized and lauded by their communities and others are left to languish in relative obscurity? What does it mean to desire recognition? Is it an unavoidable desire?

Although answers are not easy to come by, our touching reflection on these and many other questions, as we held and stroked each other, was a good start. We chatted all night and into the morning until I had to catch my plane. He decided to stay on in my hotel until the cleaning staff kicked him out. We decided not to fuck and thought we'd save that for our next eagerly anticipated time together. Sadly, that was not to be.

I still keenly recall ascending the stairs to the small airplane in Bradford, outside Leeds, a little delirious from not having slept for three days. I took note of the sky as dawn was breaking, the glowering bluish tinge, the dramatic clouds, and took a mental note to purposefully remember this image.

Sam died six months later from an accidental drug overdose. He was 21. At the time of his death, I knew that he was actively involved in an effort to raise awareness of five female sex-workers that had been murdered in Ipswich where he lived. Our intense phone, social media and yes, snail mail epistolary relationship brought us into a kind of intimate space that fuelled an excitement in both of us. Our plans to meet up in August never materialized. He overdosed while on a trip to the Canary Islands, a mere six months after our meeting and that glorious shared night in a Leeds hotel room.

Today I sometimes look at the few images that Sam sent me, one where he was sitting on his bed, nude and wearing a gas mask in profile, an object he kept hanging from a hook in the wall. His parents mailed that yellow "Children be Gay" T-shirt to me as a keepsake; it's a treasured item. I don't wear it though—it's too big for me.

My relationships with Raven and Sam in some ways created a kind of queer 'age bandits,' the feeling that we are colluding against the mainstream, and indeed in many ways we are. As one queer boy-lover once wrote, it's difficult for a young person to hold onto the typical age-graded authority towards adults in our culture once you've had a desired and consensual sexual experience with that person that amounts to a mutually respectful friendship.

Catastrophe and ecstasy—walking, twinned, in our queer souls is how we breathe, and the struggle is to upend the tight hold of fear. We need to soar in solidarity through the intimate and often life-saving vital knowledge that is transmitted between youth and the more experienced and back again through the sharing of bodily urgencies, honest mindfulness and open hearts.

Our Authors

Gordon Bowness is a writer, editor and producer living on Toronto Island with his boyfriend, Maurice Vellekoop. Bowness was the arts editor of *Xtra!*, Canada's leading LGBTQ newspaper, from 1996 to 2009, and the founding editor of two other LGBTQ publications, *Go Big* and *In Toronto* (now *In Magazine*). His current projects include a musical about *The Boho Girls*, co-written with David Christopher Richards and Lisa Lambert, and a novel, tentatively called *Prairie Orchid*, a fictional account of his mother's life.

Alec Butler is an award-winning playwright and filmmaker, one of his plays, *Black Friday*, was a finalist for the Governor General's Award for Drama in 1991. His animated video trilogy about growing up 2Spirit/Intersex/Trans called *Misadventures of Pussy Boy* has screened at numerous film festivals internationally, winning the best short/audience favourite award at the International Transgender Film Festival in Amsterdam, the Netherlands in 2013. His novella about growing up Intersex/2spirit in a rough working-class neighbourhood on the East Coast, *Rough Paradise,* was published by Quattro Books in 2014. Currently, Alec is studying towards his Master's Degree in Indigenous and Sexual Diversity Studies at the University of Toronto.

Nancy Jo Cullen's stories have appeared in *The Puritan, Prairie Fire, Grain, Plenitude, filling Station, The New Quarterly, This*

Magazine and *The Journey Prize* 24 and 26. She has published three collections of poetry with Frontenac House Press. Her most recent book, the short story collection *Canary*, is the winner of the 2012 Metcalf-Rooke Award. Nancy Jo is the 2010 winner of the Writers' Trust Dayne Ogilvie Prize for Emerging LGBTQ Writer.

Anne Fleming is the author of *Gay Dwarves of America*, a finalist for the Ethel Wilson Fiction Prize, the novel *Anomaly*, and *Pool-Hopping and Other Stories*, shortlisted for a BC Book Prize and the Governor General's Award. A book of poems, *Poemw*, will be out in 2016. She teaches creative writing at UBC's Okanagan Campus and divides her time between Kelowna and Vancouver.

RJ Gilmour spent years as a serial student in North America and Asia studying fine art, philosophy and history before graduating with a Ph.D in history from York University. A previous collection with Between the Lines press in 2012, *"Too Asian?": Race, Privilege and Post-Secondary Education*, brought together authors incensed by a Maclean's article that misrepresented Asian-Canadians. A new documentary project looks at the history of homoerotic artists and how contemporary queer artists are influenced by the works of those who came before. He lives with his partner in Toronto.

Steve MacIsaac is an expat Canadian living in Los Angeles after several years in Japan. His comic series *SHIRTLIFTER* explores contemporary gay culture, identity, and sexuality. His work has appeared in *BEST AMERICAN COMICS* 2010 (Houghton Mifflin), *NO STRAIGHT LINES* (Fantagraphics), and *QU33R* (Northwest Press). www.stevemacisaac.com

Derek McCormack is the author of the novels *The Well-Dressed Wound*, *The Show That Smells*, and *The Haunted Hillbilly*. *The Haunted Hillbilly* was nominated for a Lambda Literary Award, and was named a best book of the year by both *The Village Voice* and *The Globe and Mail.* He lives in Toronto.

Maria-Belén Ordóñez is Assistant Professor at OCAD University in the Faculty of Liberal Arts and Sciences and Interdisciplinary Studies and Digital Futures. She teaches feminist theory and ethnographic writing and is a member of FemTechNet, a network of international feminist scholars, artists and educators in New Media, Science and Technology, teaching distributed nodal courses across North America. Her most recent research is on the unravelling of the former head of the IMF, Dominique Strauss-Khan in "Circuits of Power, Labour and Desire: The Case of Dominique Strauss-Khan," in *Reworking Post Colonialism: Globalization, Labour and Rights* (London: Palgrave Macmillan, Spring 2015).

Karleen Pendleton-Jiménez is a writer and professor at Trent University. Her two books *Are You a Boy or a Girl?* and *How to Get a Girl Pregnant* were both Lambda Literary finalists. Her new book *Tomboys and Other Gender Heroes: Confessions from the Classroom* documents gender experiences of students ages 8–18 in rural Ontario. She has published numerous short stories and personal essays about lesbian desire, Latina ethnicity, and transgressive gender experience. Her award-winning film *Tomboy* has been screened around the world.

Nik Sheehan, a Canadian filmmaker, has made five critically acclaimed, widely broadcast documentary features. *FLicKeR* (2008) is the story of artist and writer Brion Gysin, made in the style of its subject. *The Drawing Master* (2005) is a *vérité* study of artist and teacher Paul Young. *God's Fool* (1997), shot in Morocco, is the story of renegade writer Scott Symons. *Symposium: Ladder of Love* (1995) revisits Plato's classic stories of the meaning of love with a cast of well-known gay Canadian artists and writers. Sheehan established an international reputation in 1985 with *No Sad Songs*, the world's first major documentary on AIDS. He lives in Vancouver.

Robert Teixeira teaches part-time at OCAD University and is completing his dissertation investigating the socio-legal governance of child and youth sexualities as a site of neoliberal regulation. He has worked as a sexual health counsellor and has been involved in community activism for many years. As a Goth kid in the 1980s, Rob has not lost his love for black clothes, which serves him well as one of the founding collective members of the Anarchist Free University in Toronto (2003–2012) where he has offered courses on queer sexual politics.

Maurice Vellekoop is an illustrator and cartoonist. His work has appeared in major magazines and advertising in North America and Europe since the 80s. He has published several books of his own work, including *The ABC Book, A Homoerotic Primer*, *Vellevision*, *Pin-ups* and *A Nut at the Opera*. He is currently at work on a graphic memoir, titled *I'm so Glad We Had this Time Together*, forthcoming from Pantheon Books (a division of Random House), New York, from which "Paul Baker: An Introduction" is an excerpt. Maurice lives with his partner Gordon Bowness on Toronto Island.

Ian Young was born in London, England in 1945. He is the author of *The Male Homosexual In Literature: A Bibliography* (Scarecrow Press), *The Stonewall Experiment: A Gay Psychohistory* (Cassell), *Sex Magick* (Stubblejumper Press) and *Out in Paperback: A Visual History of Gay Pulps* (Lester, Mason & Begg). His short stories of London life in the early 1980s have appeared in various British and U.S. anthologies, most recently *Speak My Language and Other Stories* (Robinson). "A Whiff of the Monster: Encounters with Scott Symons" is reprinted from *Encounters with Authors* (Sykes Press). He lives in Toronto with his partner Wulf.